View From Behind the Couch is dedicated to:

Deborah Herrick
For making me believe I could write it.
And
Deborah Herrick-Merkwan
For helping make it happen.

Thank You for Abusing Me
Book 1: View From Behind the Couch

Author Coleen Liebsch
Editor Deborah Merkwan
Proofreading and Formatting Quinn Editing
Cover Art James Tully

Copyright 2023 Performance Strategies Publishing
All rights reserved. This book or any portion thereof may not be reproduced or used in any manner whatsoever without the express written permission of the publisher, except for the use of brief quotations in a book review.

ISBN: 978-1-942333-30-2

Performance Strategies Publishing
100 Northbay Drive, PO Box 385
Arlington, SD 57212

www.PublishPS.com

FOREWARD

Dear Reader,

Capitalization is "required" on a variety of words in the English language. To me, it always boils down to a demonstration of respect. Therefore, a lack of capitalization, when it should be used, demonstrates a lack of respect. Please keep that in mind as you read my story.

I've changed some of the names to protect the innocent and guilty alike.

I hope you enjoy the beginning of my story!

Coleen

ABANDONED

It was 1973, and my sister Diane and I were sitting on our couch watching television. The sofa sat diagonally in the corner of our single-wide trailer house so we could see the television, the front door, and even the kitchen if we leaned over the arm of the couch far enough.

The television played *Family Affair,* and I envied Buffy's hair, her freckles, pretty much everything about her. As I dreamt of a happy home, the front door swung wide, and my father walked through the opening. He was a truck driver when we lived in that trailer, and he had been on the road a whole week.

It had been a good week.

Dad slammed the door behind him, but it was a heavy double trailer house door that had to be slammed to stay shut. My heart stopped for a moment. I couldn't read his mood.

A partial wall in front of the door blocked some of the cold air from getting into the kitchen and living room. It was large enough for a person to take off his shoes but cramped if more than one tried to come in at a time. As far as my sister and I were concerned, it was where we kicked our shoes off and left them where they landed.

As soon as she heard the door opening, Mom was drying her hands and walking toward the front door. My heart resumed its normal beat when Mom met dad at the door, and he greeted her with a kiss. Diane and I let out synchronized sighs of relief as we watched the sweet moment between our parents transpire.

It was nice to have dad home … when he was happy.

For a moment, I thought maybe we could be like a normal family, but when dad stepped back from the kiss, he spat in Mom's face.

Dad hadn't noticed Diane or me, as we scrambled into our hiding place behind the couch. I peeked around the corner to see dad grab a handful of Mom's long blonde hair and yank her out of the shoe room. He used her hair like a leash to pull her through the four feet of living room and ten feet of kitchen. I saw when Mom fell by the sink, and I saw him pull her by her hair into the back hallway, never letting her on her feet.

Our parents were out of sight, but we heard every sound. The dull thud of an object from the bathroom hitting Mom in the head. The sharp stinging sound of a slap to Mom's face. The loud thump that shook the trailer when dad slammed Mom into the bathroom wall.

For the next several hours we listened as dad beat Mom and screamed horrible words at her. Mom didn't know what started the fight any more than Diane or I did, and she begged him to stop and tell her what was wrong.

When the screaming and pleading finally ended, my sister looked at me and said, "Mom's dead."

I was seven years old.

The only sounds from the back of the house were the wailing cries of our terrified baby brother, Mark.

Diane wanted me to go back to see what was going on, but I was too scared. I didn't have a reason to go back and talk to them. Dad would know I'd been listening. But my paralyzing fear wasn't just about being caught eavesdropping. I was terrified of what I might find.

"Just tell them you have a stomachache," Diane suggested.

It wasn't a lie. I did have a stomachache. My mind raced as I played out scenarios of what I might find. Tears welled in my eyes because none of the scenarios had good endings.

My fear didn't change the matter at hand. Someone had to go back there, and my sister was positively not going to do it.

I took a deep breath and summoned enough courage to stand from my hiding place behind the couch. I turned sideways to fit through the space between the arm of the couch and the wall. My eyes stayed focused on the opening to the dark hallway beyond the kitchen. I wished and prayed with all my might it would be dad I would find dead, but I knew that would be too good to be true.

I walked into the kitchen, propelled by the beat of my heart. The dark hallway loomed just a few steps away. The purple shag carpet, wood paneling, and the lack of windows made the hallway darker than it needed to be, but I could see a light shining out into the hallway at the end. Waiting at the end of the hall was the object of my nightmares.

I froze at the entrance of the long dark tunnel.

I could hold my breath to keep quiet, but I was sure my pounding heart would give me away before I even took a step. I wished and prayed for the darkness to end, but I couldn't turn on the light. Dad would see.

Mark's cries had become quiet sobs, but the light was still off in the bedroom. No one had gone in to soothe him, and he had been crying for a really, long time. That was a bad sign.

The light from the bathroom at the end of the hallway would have to be enough to guide my steps. After a hopeful look back to see if my sister might have changed her mind, I took my first step.

Alone.

Slowly and carefully, on my tiptoes so nothing would creak and give me away, I took a few more steps. By my fourth step the hallway seemed to be narrowing in on me. The ceiling seemed almost within reach, and yet the doorway to the bathroom seemed to be moving further away.

All my father had to do was peek out from whichever door he was behind, and he would catch me.

The door to the bedroom I shared with Diane was on my left but closed. I considered sneaking into my room and into the closet where no one could ever find me during hide-and-seek. My heart begged my hands to reach for the door, but I kept my head down and walked on.

Anxiety tightened its grip, and my heart beat faster. The endless hallway was coming to an end as my baby steps brought me just a step away from the bathroom door.

I braced myself for the last step that would put me in the doorway. The moment he would know I was there. The moment I would know what happened to Mom. As much as I wanted to be out of the darkness, the bright light streaming out would illuminate everything I didn't want to see.

I took a deep breath and stepped into the doorway.

Dad was leaning against the wall. His head was buried in his arms, as if he had his head down on a desk instead of up against the wall. My heart sank when I realized my prayers for his death had gone unanswered. He never took his head out of his arms to see me enter the bathroom. He was in the "I'm sorry" stage.

Ceramic fish that were once wall decorations were shattered across the floor and in the tub. Those were the dull thuds that hit Mom's head. They were all spattered with blood.

More blood dripped on the walls, on the toilet, and on the edge of the tub. Mom was leaning against the sink, and I could see her reflection in the mirror that hung above it. Fortunately, the mirror was intact so we wouldn't have seven years of bad luck.

Mom was pressing a wet washcloth against her left eye, but her other hand was dabbing toilet paper against a hundred other cuts that were still dripping blood. She was hurt, but she was alive!

I no longer cared what dad was doing or how he might react. Mom was alive, and I was just a few feet away—I could almost touch her. I closed the space between us. I wanted to hug her or comfort her in some way. Instead, I stood there like an idiot and said, "I have a stomachache."

Mom opened the mirror that hid a medicine cabinet only grown-ups could reach and handed me a bottle of Pepto-Bismol. She told me how much to take and immediately went back to work on her face.

As I took the bottle I searched my mind, desperately trying to come up with a reason to stay with Mom, in case the monster inside my father awoke again.

Neither Mom nor dad looked at me or asked questions. Dad's face remained buried in his arms and Mom tended to her face. With nothing left to say, I walked slowly out of the room.

I had no courage left. Instead of helping Mom, I had made the moment about me and my make-believe stomachache. I complained about something ridiculously petty when my mother had just been beaten to a bloody pulp! I left without helping her. I had left my mother alone with the monster.

In a daze, I tried to process everything I'd seen. Before I knew it, I was at the kitchen sink pouring medicine into a teaspoon. It never occurred to me not to take it as Mom instructed. Diane was at my side as I spooned the liquid into my mouth.

"What did you see?" I could see the stress and anxiety—that nearly made my own heart explode—distorting my sister's face. I reported every tiny detail and watched as Diane's anguish turned to relief. Relief I should have felt but couldn't. All I could feel was guilt over abandoning my mom when she needed me most.

THE GOOD OLE DAYS

We had only been asleep a few hours when I awoke to a knock on the front door. I looked through the window and saw my mom's parents!

It was the middle of winter, so Grandpa Olson waited in the running Pontiac with my aunt Lily, my mom's sister with Down Syndrome. I could never quite figure out Lily's relationship within the family because she called Grandpa "Dad" but called Grandma "Mabel."

Lily was born in 1939 in a small hospital in rural South Dakota. At that time, parents were not allowed to raise handicapped children at home. They were immediately sent to the State School and Home for the Feeble Minded in Redfield. The hospital not only held newborn babies with Down Syndrome, it also housed the criminally insane.

After Lily was born, the doctor told my grandfather the powers that be were on their way to take her Lily to the state hospital. My grandpa replied, "The hell you are." He then took his wife and newborn baby home to their farm where Lily would spend almost all her life.

The issue didn't end there, however. My grandparents were forced into court to defend their right to raise their baby at home. When the judge ruled in their favor, he added, "Don't ever expect any help from the state." And my grandfather would not. Even after services became available to integrate Lily into jobs and social situations, Grandpa would have none of it.

No one ever explained Lily's condition to me. All I knew was she was a grown up in charge when Grandma and Grandpa weren't around—and she was mean!

In addition to Down Syndrome, Lily had a terrible stutter that caused her to use catch phrases rather than sentences. If there was something she didn't want to do, eat, say, whatever, her reply would always be, "Not for me."

The worst thing about Lily was that Diane and I had to sleep with her when we stayed at their farm. Since I was the youngest, I had to sleep in the middle, which meant I was always within Lily's reach.

Lying under a pile of Grandma's thick quilts felt like heaven until Lily crawled in next to me. I tried to fall asleep, but I could feel her watching me, even with my eyes closed. Sometimes I opened them, just to see her staring at me as a devious smile spread across her face. I knew what she was doing; she was waiting for me to fall asleep.

Somewhere along the line, Lily decided children loved to be tickled. Without fail, the minute I fell asleep, Lily would wake me by digging her bony fingers into my rib cage.

There was no way to control my involuntary reaction and I laughed, which reinforced her belief it was something I enjoyed. It didn't matter that tears were running down my face, or that I was begging her to stop. She just kept tickling me, for hours, until she decided the game was over.

When it wasn't bedtime, though, the Olson farm was magical.

It never occurred to me to ask what my grandparents did for a living. I assumed they were farmers because they had food growing as far as I could see.

Between the house and garage lay a beautiful flower garden with every flower imaginable. Behind the garage was the rhubarb patch, and across from that began a huge row sectioned off for strawberries, carrots, peas, beans, radishes, and melons. Up against the old shed were the raspberries, and from there all the way to

Grandpa's other field was sweet corn. The field behind the granary was for sweetcorn too and was so big Grandpa had to use his tractor to reach the end of it.

Days were filled with chores, and I "helped" Grandpa with them all. Whether that meant swimming in oats while Grandpa filled feed buckets, exploring shelter belts while he hoed weeds, or caring for baby animals we found along the way, if we were visiting, I was with Grandpa. Visiting the Olson farm was like returning to the "Good Ole" days. Neighbors looked out for each other, and everyone knew everyone else.

Every day Grandma lovingly tended to the plants until fall when she canned everything from the garden for use during the long winter.

Nothing went to waste at the Olson house. Watermelon rind became the most delicious, sweet pickles. Old Pringles cans became nail sorters in Grandpa's workshop. Old milk cartons became tomato planters, and old nylon stockings became the filling of the most amazing quilts in the world.

Everything mattered at the Olson farm, including me.

But Lily was never left alone; and now she waited in the car with Grandpa who, truth be told, didn't much care for my dad.

When I entered the kitchen, I noticed my colorful orange and red paisley suitcase by the door. I had completely forgotten we were going to stay with Grandma and Grandpa. My sister's blue and purple paisley suitcase and my brother's diaper bag sat on either side of mine. All three had been gifts from Grandma and Grandpa Olson. I wondered when Mom had packed my suitcase.

And then the big question hit me. What would happen when our secret was exposed? Grandma would see the cuts and bruises on Mom's face! She would find out about the secret monster who lived in our house!

Mom greeted Grandma at the front door, and I held my breath as I heard my grandmother's words in her thick Norwegian accent.

"Ooftah! What happened to you?" Her voice was filled with concern.

Mom told an elaborate story about falling down the stairs while bringing groceries into the house. We did have a rickety wooden stairway that led up to our trailer house, and it was icy, but there were only two steps. Would Grandma believe someone could really get injuries like that from falling two steps into snow? Mom looked like a boxer the day after losing a fight. Grandma never questioned Mom's story; she just held Mom's face in her hands as she inspected the damage up close.

We'd never been told the things happening inside our home were secret, but somehow, we knew. As it turns out, domestic violence is an incredibly easy secret to keep.

When Mom said it was time for us to go—and it was clear she wasn't coming along—I panicked. I was positive he would hurt her even worse than he already had, and we wouldn't be there to help! We couldn't leave her alone with the monster.

I hugged Mom's legs and cried. "Please, please don't make me go to Grandma and Grandpa's. I want to stay here with you."

"But you love to go out to the farm. Why wouldn't you want to go?" Mom asked. I had no answer. I couldn't say I was afraid dad would kill her.

I couldn't say I had to stay home to scan my room for weapons in case things became bad again. Instead, I said something I will always regret.

"It's boring there." The look of sadness on my favorite grandma's face was horrible. I had made her sad with my lie. Grandma and Grandpa Olson's farm was my happy place. Even as a child, I knew the memories made there would become my good ol' days in the future. I watched my words break my grandmother's heart.

NO CHANCE IN HELL

I spent hundreds of hours trying to figure out what kinds of things set my father off. What was the common denominator that made him go from being a fun-loving guy to a person who could pound a defenseless mother of three? If answers existed, I had to find them. He wasn't always a monster, so there had to be something...

I already knew how to protect myself from the monsters under my bed. I'd known that for as long as I could remember. I knew what set them off. I knew the rules.

Rule number 1: Make sure every part of my body is on top of the bed. If anything hung over the edge, like an arm or part of my pajamas, the monsters could grab it.

Rule number 2: Always stay covered by at least one sheet. The head and face were an exception, of course, unless the monster was truly dreadful.

Rule number 3: Make absolutely no sound when the dreadful monsters were around.

Now, I'm no monster expert, but those rules always worked for me. No monsters ever came out from under my bed. They all walked in through the door.

I don't remember learning to tiptoe around my father, or when I started to study him to figure out what set him off. Those feelings, that knowledge, were just always there. Because dad's anger was always there.

I was born in 1966, when the kitchen tables had Formica coverings that looked like marble, only to be given away by their aluminum frame. The matching chairs had plastic seats and back rests with a marble design to match the tabletop. The shiny aluminum frames of the table and chairs became sharp when things smashed against the light metal. There was never a time in my life when those aluminum edges weren't sharp.

My sister Diane was two and a half when I was born, and she was practically perfect in everyone's eyes. She was cute, precocious, and good at everything she tried. I, on the other hand, came out looking like my football-shaped head had been attached sideways.

"When you were born," Mom recounted, "you had red hair that stood up about an inch high all over your head. I asked the nurses to comb it down with some Vaseline, but they said they couldn't do that. They said I could do whatever I wanted to your hair when I took you home, but they couldn't put anything in your hair at the hospital. 'Then, no pictures,' I had told them." The first picture of me was taken when I was about four months old.

From what I've been told, the moment my parents put me into a crib I scooted back and forth all day long. They chose the obvious nickname "Scooter," which was, for many years, the only name I knew I had.

Like most parents, I'm sure Mom wondered if she could possibly love a second child as much as she loved her first. "I wanted to make sure your sister didn't feel less important after you were born, so I only ever played with you when she was asleep," Mom said. "I would say things like 'That naughty baby messed her diaper again.' I realized I was getting carried away with it when Diane pulled me aside and said, 'Don't you love our baby?'"

In fairness, I was an ugly child. My cheeks were too wide, and my smile literally split my face from ear to ear. My hair was wild, and my eyes were too close together. A troll doll wouldn't be an unfair comparison.

For almost three years my sister had been the only grandchild on both sides and loved being the center of attention. Whether it was showing people how she danced and sang, or demonstrating her cartwheels in the yard, there was always someone to take photos and videos. Her baby book was full. Diane inherited her love of the spotlight from dad. I inherited my love of animals.

From as early as I can remember, my best friends were animals. I had broken my toe just before my first birthday when a can of soup fell on my foot in the grocery cart. For that reason, I didn't take my first steps until around eighteen months, and they were straight toward our dog Teeny. Just before my second birthday, Teeny had six puppies!

Perhaps because of my broken toe—or maybe to keep me out of her way—Mom frequently put me on the bed with the puppies. I loved lying on my back as the puppies bounced all over my torso and climbed across my arms and legs. My favorite part was when they licked my face.

"Ewwwww!" Diane would yell as soon as the kisses hit my mouth, but I didn't care. I loved every one of my puppies. As the babies grew bigger, I didn't stand a chance walking, or even sitting up, when the puppies came running and pounced on me. My sister may have had people friends, but I had the best friends in the whole world tackle me with kisses every day.

One day a lady knocked on our door. When Mom opened the door, I saw a woman I didn't recognize walk in and start playing with my puppies. She picked each one up and looked it over before putting it back down on the floor. As she set each puppy down, I checked it over for potential injuries. I didn't understand any of the things my mom and the lady talked about, but then the woman picked up one of my puppies, and she left with it!

One after another, my puppies were given away until only Teeny remained. My best friend and I were alone again.

Eventually, Teeny and I developed a routine that didn't involve puppies.

One day, while my best friend and I sat on the living room floor playing with some toys and my mother sat at the table clipping coupons, someone knocked on the door.

The only thing separating our living room from the dining room where Mom sat was our couch. It was a 1960s contemporary style with scratchy fabric and hard sides that hurt when you bumped your head on them. Teeny sat next to me on the floor, and we both looked up as Mom rose from the table.

The knocking had turned Teeny into a barking machine, so Mom picked her up before answering the door. I crawled to the couch, which faced away from the table, and used the piping around the couch to pull myself up. I saw a woman who looked familiar.

"Would you care for a cup of coffee?" Mom asked as she held Teeny in one arm.

"That would be great, thank you." Then this woman said, "I just can't believe the puppy is dead." She covered her eyes and began to cry.

I knew what dead was and, in that moment, I also remembered who the woman was. I'd spent enough time on my grandparents' farm to know you can't bring dead things into the house, and when they're outside long enough, their bottom side will be covered with maggots.

I glared at the horrible woman who had taken one of Teeny's puppies as my mom told the woman everything was going to be alright.

"It was so stupid! I *always* close the cistern cap when the water truck leaves. I just feel so bad that I wasn't there to stop the puppy from falling in."

I knew what cisterns were.

She had let my puppy fall into the water.

My Grandma Olson had been terrified of someone falling into the cistern tank ever since my mom was a child. She pointed it out to me at the start of every visit.

"Now make sure you don't get close to the cistern tank or the ground around it," Grandma would warn my sister and me. "If you fall in that tank, there's no way to get you out, and it's full of water."

That was all it took to scare me away from the cistern cap. I'd never even seen the actual hole it covered.

This woman wasn't even smart enough to put the cap back on the hole!

When Mom returned to the table with the woman's coffee, she set Teeny on the woman's lap before taking her own chair. The woman oohed and ahhhed over my dog as she stroked Teeny's fur from head to tail.

I did not want her touching my dog.

It made me even madder that Teeny liked the woman! My best friend was licking the face of a woman who had killed one of her babies, and she didn't even know it! The betrayal fueled my anger and for the first time, I felt true hatred. I hated the woman who sat at our kitchen table with my mom.

It wasn't very long before the woman stood and gave my mom a hug. She was still holding my dog. She apologized for the way things turned out but wished Mom luck.

She didn't give my dog back.

She didn't set Teeny down.

I used the piping of the couch to pull myself along faster than I could walk, but all I could do was watch as the horrible lady walked out the door. She still had my dog!

My screams and cries fell on deaf ears as I tried to explain to my mom that a horrible woman was stealing my dog, but I was barely two years old. No one thought to explain to a fussy toddler what was happening.

The woman never brought Teeny back, and it wasn't long before Mom packed our things to move. Our big house, with the private screening room in our closet, was furnished, so packing mostly meant clothes and toys. As we drove away from the best place I'd ever lived, I cried and wondered how Teeny would ever find me after we moved.

She never did.

***

Dad left truck driving when his regionally popular band got a long-term gig. In those days, groups were hired to be "house bands" who would play four or five nights each week for months on end. Sometimes the band knew how long a gig would last; sometimes it ended suddenly. It almost always ended with us moving to the next gig.

It was 1968 when we moved to Big Stone, South Dakota. Six months later a gig took us to Ortonville, Minnesota. As the sixties came to an end, so did dad's gig. The next one took us to Livingston, Montana.

Diane and I weren't usually in the bars while dad's band played, but we were always there for setup and sound check. Chairs were always upside down on top of the tables, like memorials to a graveyard of parties gone by.

"Keep your shoes on," Mom would always say when Diane and I wanted to explore. Neither of us needed to ask why.

Each step we took was tacky, as our shoes stuck just a little bit to the carpeted floor. I wondered if the carpet had always been flat, or if crowds of people smashed it down over time. Either way, my sister and I were happy to explore under tables for treasures abandoned after the last party.

When the stage lights came on, the thick haze of smoke that hung above my head danced and swirled around the room. From my vantage point below the fog, it was beautiful. It was in those smoke-hazed lights where my father was at his best.

One of dad's greatest talents was being able to imitate famous artists. Whether it was Johnny Cash or Elvis, dad didn't just sound like them, he took on their mannerisms. The ladies in the lounge swooned over my father in his gold lamé suit and rarely paid attention to his wife or children watching from some booth in the back.

While the tables might be different shapes or sizes, and the bartender area might be in a different spot of the room, the bars all looked the same. We had already lived in four different towns by the time I was three, but Livingston was one of my favorites.

Once we reached our new destination—an old house that had been divided into two apartments—I unpacked my red and orange paisley suitcase while Diane unpacked her blue and green one. We were home.

The best part was that it didn't matter in what town our driveway was located—my best friend was always waiting in the yard when I finished unpacking.

Her name was Missy, and both her parents were in dad's band. Her father was the steel guitar player, and her mom sang backup and played bass. They lived in an old school bus converted into an RV on the inside. On the outside, different sections of panels were painted various colors. Missy and her parents were a permanent fixture outside whatever dwelling we happened to be renting, so moving never bothered me a bit.

Inside our apartment house, I found another best friend who lived in the upstairs apartment. Her father was in dad's band as well, but I don't remember the instrument he played. He was quiet and rarely around if we kids were present.

The neighborhood was literally crawling with kids in the same age range as my sister and me. Diane was five, I was three, and Mark wouldn't be along for another few years.

Between practices, brainstorming, and just plain old drinking sessions, our house was constantly buzzing with musicians, friends, and neighbors. Those times were good. Dad was always nicer when other people were around.

One of our visitors was a man we called Harold Parold." He was the youngest of dad's bandmates and both Diane and I dreamed about growing up and marrying him. He was a fill-in guitarist, so we only saw Harold a few times each year, but I imagined he spent the rest of his life in glamorous locations. Places far better than where we lived.

Since Harold was single, he slept on a fold-up cot in our closet. When married people stayed with us, my sister and I had to move to the couch; but until I grew up and married him, Harold was stuck on the cot.

One night I walked up to Harold Parold—who was tucked into his cot—to tell him good night. He must have shifted in just the wrong way because that bed folded right in half on him! It was the funniest thing I'd ever seen!

Then there was Russ. He wasn't in the band, and I don't even know how he and my father became friends. Russ was Native American and came to stay with us whenever he was released from jail and had nowhere else to go. He always slept on the couch because he sometimes had to leave in the middle of the night. Every time he came to visit, he brought Diane and me games *and* candy. He was our favorite houseguest.

One night when Russ was sleeping on the couch, we all awoke to bloodcurdling screams from the living room. He had sleepwalked onto the big grate Mom told us never to touch—a burning-hot furnace vent in the center of the room. By the time we saw him, Russ was awake and off the grate, waving his arms and jumping from foot to foot as he screamed like he was crazy. It was even funnier than seeing Harold folded up in the bed.

That one vent heated our whole apartment so, when the heat was on, it glowed red hot. It even melted our Halloween bags one year.

In the morning, Russ showed us the waffle pattern branded onto the bottoms of both his feet, and I felt bad for laughing at his pain. That was until dad started in on him.

Russ's midnight dance shouldn't have seemed funny to any of us after seeing his injuries, but we couldn't help giggling out loud when dad made fun of his Native American friend's "rain dance." Dad jumped back and forth from one foot to the other as he patted his mouth and chanted, "Hi, howareya, hi, howareya."

Even Russ, with his feet still stinging in pain, couldn't help but laugh.

That was one of my father's great talents—the ability to turn something that would get someone else in trouble to his own benefit. It was probably the thing I hated most about him, even when I was three.

None of our houseguests ever seemed to consider their "wonderful guy" could be a monster at home. He was different around them. He would do anything in the world, any time of the day, for any of his friends. Why was he so different with us?

Maybe we were the source of his frustration, the imperfect baggage keeping him from a life of greater things, the power short in his spotlight.

To me, my father was just scary. Most of his physical abuse was aimed at Mom and Diane, but not knowing what set him off meant I had no chance in hell of protecting them ... or myself.

SWALLOWING MY GUILT

The bathroom in our ground floor apartment was on the exact opposite wall as the front door, which meant that from the bathroom doorway you could see the whole living/dining room, along with the doors to the bedrooms. What you couldn't see from the bathroom doorway was the kitchen. Even at age three, I knew that meant Mom wouldn't be able to see me either.

I started out with normal intentions, but when I walked into the bathroom, I saw dad's razor sitting on the sink. It was the kind you unscrew from the handle to expose a two-sided razor blade. I turned the handle back and forth, opening and closing the lid of the razor, fascinated by its mechanisms. It wasn't long before the temptation of the shiny blade overtook me. How in the world did it fit in and out of its slot?

I took the blade out of the trick door I'd been opening and closing, then turned the blade back and forth in my fingers. I was surprised at how bendy the metal seemed to be, but for the life of me I could not figure out how to get the blade back into position in the razor.

A shadow crossed into my peripheral vision, and I instinctively tossed the blade and razor into the basin of the sink. My hands went behind my back and found each other in a clasp.

I hadn't noticed blood dripping onto the floor.

"What are you doing?" dad sked. He was mad. He grabbed my hands and pulled them toward him, which caused blood to splatter around the tiny bathroom.

"What were you doing?" he raged.

"Nothing," I said, my eyes wide and my fingertips dripping blood.

"Were you playing with my razor?" Dad was bent over, asking the question in my face as he held onto my wounded fingers.

I knew I'd better have a good answer, or I was going to be in big trouble.

"No," I cleverly replied.

"Then why are your hands bleeding?"

I was busted.

My mind raced as I tried to come up with some reason I was bleeding—any reason at all—other than playing with a razor blade. That's when I saw my dog walk by.

"Spotty bit me," I said quietly without looking into my father's face.

I thought blaming Spotty would be a free pass for everyone. Dad couldn't possibly blame the dog. He told me all the time that dogs will nip when they're playing. Dad wouldn't punish Spotty.

I was wrong.

Spotty wandered in at the sound of his name. Out of nowhere, dad kicked him out of the bathroom and across the dining area. Dad's cowboy boots clomped on the hard floor as he stormed out to where Spotty landed and kicked him again. Spotty yelped as the pointed toe of dad's cowboy boot landed blow after blow until Spotty stopped moving.

I stood in the doorway to the bathroom and watched helplessly as my father tortured my puppy over my lie. When dad stormed out the front door, I ran to Spotty. He had crawled under the table, and I crawled next to him, trying to comfort him.

He was whimpering but whined louder if I tried to put my arm on him. He hurt everywhere, and it was my fault. I had lied and it was Spotty who was punished for it. I told him over and over again how sorry I was, but it didn't matter. The damage was done.

The cuts on my fingers eventually healed, but Spotty's injuries never would. He died that night under the table, at my side.

That may have been the moment my father realized the best way to hurt me was to hurt others I cared about—or maybe customizing punishments came as easily to my father as winning people over.

The motivation was irrelevant. The outcome was the same: I was guilty of causing someone else's pain.

NEW FEAR UNLOCKED

One of my father's biggest supporters was a woman named Donna, who occasionally sang harmonies in his band. Whether it was because he had given her a job or some other reason, Donna worshipped the ground my father walked upon.

Donna was beautiful. Her long blonde hair was always perfectly piled atop her head, intricate swirls with strands hanging down in the perfect places. Her eyelashes were long, dark, and as thick as the rest of the makeup on her face, but it all made her look flawless.

She always wore sexy mini skirt outfits that accentuated her legs, which were longer than I was tall. And she always wore go-go boots, also longer than I was tall. She never wore heels shorter than four inches. In fact, I remember the night she called in sick for a show because she had fallen off her shoes and broken her leg. I wondered how she would have felt about dad if she knew how many times he had joked about her inability to walk on her own two feet.

One night in the early seventies we were staying at my father's parents' house. Grandpa Ned and Grandma Naomi were the exact opposite of my mother's parents. It wasn't just that they lived in town and the Olsons lived in the country. No, it really boiled down to one thing: Grandma Mable appreciated everything, and Grandma Naomi appreciated nothing.

One time we were staying with my paternal grandparents after a show. Sometime in the middle of the night Donna showed up on Grandma's doorstep in the middle of the night, crying. Her long blonde hair was still perfectly teased on top of her head, but her cheeks were streaked with black. The tears streaming down her face were black with mascara, but I'd seen worse. To me she was still the same beautiful woman from the band posters. She just needed to wash her face.

Donna and her boyfriend had been in a fight, and she had come to my father for help. Diane and I weren't allowed in the room while the grownups smoked Pall Malls and listened to the story of Donna's tragic evening. It didn't matter that we weren't allowed in the kitchen. I could hear everything. She was telling her own story about a monster ... to a guy who was a monster himself. And she didn't even know it!

I listened as dad offered to beat the abusive boyfriend to a pulp. I listened as dad called her boyfriend terrible names. I wondered why he didn't think those same names applied to him. Even as a kid I despised hypocrisy, and it made me hate him even more.

It was the middle of the night in a small town, and Grandma Naomi's biggest concern was that one of her neighbors might gossip about whose car was parked in front of her house. But Grandma could never say no to my dad. They invited the singer to stay ... but just for the night.

Donna took the overnight bag she'd brought along into the one and only bathroom in my grandparents' house. I remember she was in there a really, really, long time—time goes very slowly when you're three and you need to pee.

When the door finally opened, a short brunette lady with little, tiny eyelashes and a cropped pixie haircut came out. Nothing about her resembled the woman I knew as Donna, and I had to peek around in the bathroom to see if the woman I knew was hiding somewhere. She wasn't.

Everything special about Donna was lying in a pile on the bathroom floor. She wasn't the person I thought she was at all. Everything people loved about her was phony.

She was just like my dad.

I had fantasized about her glamorous life. I had imagined her living in a sparkling world of spotlights and autographs, in an apartment overlooking a beautiful skyline. But after the spotlight went dark, the life she went home to wasn't any better than ours.

A few months after Donna showed up at my grandparents' door in the middle of the night, I overheard my parents talking. Donna had killed herself. Her life was more than she could deal with; but from what I'd seen of it, her situation was a fraction of the ordeal Mom faced on a near-daily basis.

A new fear popped into my three-year-old brain. What if Mom decided killing herself was the best way out for her?

I'd always been afraid dad might kill her someday, but the idea that my mom could kill herself doubled the odds of losing her. Nightmares of Mom's death invaded my sleep. I couldn't articulate my fears, so I found as many ways as I could to keep Mom by my side. One of them was my bedtime routine.

My long hair, which helped cover my football-shaped head, had been matted together with gum more than one morning, so Mom had taken to checking my mouth for gum before bed. I made a game out of flattening the squishy delicacy to fit across the roof of my mouth or tucking it far back behind where my teeth stopped. I giggled at the idea of pulling one over on my mother and smirked as she used her finger to dig around inside my mouth.

The prize for winning that game of hide and seek was a pixie haircut that jolted me back into the category of ugliest kid on the block.

Good or bad, Mom was the one who took care of us all. Not just my sister and me, but the other band members' children too. It didn't matter how little we had; Mom always figured out a way to help anyone who was worse off than we were.

The scary nights were only bearable because of Mom. With my new fear of Mom's death unlocked, I began to wish for my father's death instead.

HARD FOOTSTEPS TO FOLLOW

There were thousands of ways Mom demonstrated her generosity and kindness, but never more than with dad's band mates.

Harold the Second was a phenomenal steel guitar player and an on-again, off-again member of dad's band. Like most of the others, he crashed at our house on more than one occasion. Usually, he only stayed with us the night of a show, but since I had no interest in marrying him, I knew nothing about his personal life. It never occurred to me he might have a family somewhere. I was mostly still irritated that he replaced my favorite Harold—Harold Parold.

As it turned out, Harold's entire family of seven depended on his income as a fill-in steel guitar player. I overheard him asking to borrow money from dad.

Dad was never one to admit when he had nothing, so he gave Harold a few dollars here and there when there was something left over from his bar tab at the end of his show.

Whenever our upstairs neighbor could keep an eye on us, Mom joined dad at the club. As a little kid, I thought it was because she was his biggest fan. As an adult, I learned she convinced the bar managers to allow her to wait tables for tips. It was the only way she could ensure any of the money from dad's gigs made it into our home.

Mom was adept at making something out of nothing. She bought bags of cereal that were as tall as I was. She bought our food from the "price reduced" section of the bargain grocery store. She collected Gold Stamps and cut out coupons to save every nickel she could.

Then one day ... she didn't.

It was obvious when we walked into the discount grocery store that it would be a different shopping trip than we were used to. For one thing, Mom grabbed the big cart that only rich people needed for their shopping. The next thing that struck me as odd was that Mom put two different boxes of cereal—not ten pound bags, actual boxes of name-brand cereal—into the cart next to me. I looked at my mother as if she had been drinking, but she just smiled as she shopped.

We continued down aisle after aisle, filling the cart with everything we were never allowed to buy. There were boxes of potato chips, packages of hamburger, and even a gallon of milk. It wasn't the kind that came in a powder and had to be shaken for a long, long time. It was real milk! We were never allowed to have those things.

I watched as the clerk bagged everything, thinking about what I was going to eat first. As Mom paid the bill in cash, I made my decision ... potato chips!

But when we left the store, we didn't go home. We drove to the apartment where Harold and his family lived. Diane held the doors as Mom carried the bags of groceries into the small apartment. If I remember correctly, I was trying to salvage whatever I could from the bags. I could salvage nothing.

I watched as Mom unpacked all the groceries she'd just purchased and stacked them into Harold the Second's empty cupboards.

Mom never said a word about it afterwards. When she gave something, it was given.

Regardless of where we lived or who lived with us, Mom welcomed each new person with Norwegian hospitality and open arms. She had every reason in the world to hate them by association, but she didn't.

I started to realize my mother's tremendous capacity for forgiveness and acceptance.

Maybe that was why, no matter how many horrible names dad called her or how many times he hurt her, Mom never called dad anything but his name. Mom was strong and beautiful, and I was convinced her life would have been just like Mary Tyler Moore's if she didn't have to put up with my father … if she wasn't bound to him by us.

Mom deserved so much more than she received, and yet she was thankful for whatever she received. It didn't matter how little we had; she would always find a way to help someone who had less. She taught me a valuable lesson.

Me? I just wanted the potato chips.

TOUGHEN UP

Regardless how much extra work my father created for my mother, between his own shenanigans and those of his couch-surfing bandmates, it was still nothing compared to the amount of work I caused the poor woman.

I was a fragile, sickly toddler who tried to keep up with her older sister and failed miserably.

Shortly before my fourth birthday, we were visiting friends in an apartment complex. Well, everyone else was visiting friends. My parents were visiting with other grown-ups who didn't want me around, and my sister was playing with the friends she had from when we lived there two years earlier. To them, I was still a baby, and they didn't want me around. They couldn't hide for long though.

I found Diane and her friend Kathy laughing and jumping up and down outside of the apartment building. I couldn't wait to find out what was so exciting!

Between two of the buildings was a space where water had run off the roofs and joined the two buildings together with a giant ice slide. My sister and her friend had been boosting each other up onto the huge block of ice, then sliding down off the end.

It was too big for me.

Diane assured me she and her friend would catch me just as I came off the end. They also assured me you hardly slipped at all. You mostly had to scoot yourself down the ice.

"Don't worry," they said. "We'll catch you."

A few hours later, the doctor was finishing the last wrap of my new cast. I had broken my arm when neither my sister nor her friend Kathy had made any move toward catching me as I flew down the giant icicle they had tossed me onto.

The plaster cast held my arm in a permanently bent position, and it weighed a ton. The doctor gave me a blue sling covered in pictures of little boys doing little boy activities. He didn't have any pink ones left, and I'd never been more disappointed in my life.

I don't remember my broken arm ever hurting, but I remember it itched like crazy. I was constantly in trouble for trying to poke things like silverware down my cast, which meant I worked hardest at it when Mom wasn't looking.

The only thing I had access to without Mom noticing was my watercolor paint set. There was a long paintbrush and little plastic compartments filled with every color in the rainbow. I stabbed the wooden tip of my paint brush as far down my cast as it would reach and it was heaven, for a while.

The thing about itches is that once you start chasing them, they run away. It seemed like my worst itches were just out of the brush's reach. That's when I figured out that popping one of the paint sections out of its compartment would give me an extra inch of itch room. The only problem was that I just had one set of paints and never thought to put the brush up the other way.

Finally, six weeks passed, and it was time to have my cast removed.

I don't remember the doctor cutting my cast with the saw, but I do remember his face when he pulled the two sides of the plaster cast apart. The stodgy old doctor went completely white. He'd gone from being kind of bossy to stuttering and saying, "I, I don't know how it could look like that. Has the child's arm been reinjured in some way?"

I looked down at my arm and was mesmerized by the colors. The spot where I'd broken my arm was purple and blue and every other color in the rainbow. It was beautiful!

The doctor pulled at it, turned it over and twisted it, all the while asking me if it hurt.

With each twist and every turn, I answered, "No."

The doctor went to the sink and held a washcloth under warm water. He brought it back over to the table to wipe the plaster dust from my arm and get a better look at my deformity. He touched the warm washcloth on my arm very gently, so as not to do any more damage. He took the first swipe of the rag across my arm, then he started to press harder. His eyes twinkled as he looked over his reading glasses at me and asked, "Did you put anything in your cast?"

"Yeeeessssss," I answered. I was far too stupid to lie.

"What did you put in there?"

I gave him the complete rundown of everything I'd put in there from knitting needles to popsicle sticks to my sister's school pencils to ... He stopped me when I mentioned my paints. In unison, the doctor and my mother asked how I got the paint down there.

"I just poked it down," I answered, as I made a poking-down motion with my finger.

The doctor scrubbed the rest of my horrific bruising away, along with the plaster. Nothing had ever felt as good as the terry cloth scratching against those six-week-old itches.

The doctor x-rayed my arm again to make sure the break had healed properly. He clipped the negative to a light and showed me the lighter patch of bone where it had grown back together. "Now that spot is the strongest spot in your arm," he told me. "You can't break a bone in the same place twice."

The doctor's advice to my mother was simple. "You just need to let her roughhouse with the other kids. You're babying her too much."

Even at three, I understood what the doctor was saying. I needed to toughen up to have any hope of being a normal kid.

ROSES AND PIGS

While my sister Diane was good at everything, I was equally bad at everything. I was uncoordinated, underweight, and just all-around sickly. It shouldn't have come as a huge surprise that I came down with the mumps during one of the most important times in Mom's life.

We were still living in Montana when my Aunt Linda asked Mom to be the Matron of Honor at her wedding. The ceremony would take place in South Dakota, but since dad still didn't care for Mom's family very much, if she wanted to go to the wedding she would have to go alone. Through nothing short of Herculean effort, that is exactly what she did.

The only way we could afford to travel was by train, so with a four- and a six-year-old in tow, Mom lugged our suitcases—long before anyone thought to put wheels on them—to the station to catch our cross-country passenger train.

As we waited in the station for our train to arrive, I spiked a fever of 104 degrees. And yes, my mother did always have a thermometer in her purse. What she didn't have that day was aspirin. It was 1970, so people didn't worry about lawsuits. When a stranger noticed Mom's situation, the lady gave her two aspirins.

I remember walking a very, very long time up a winding ramp. All the windows were a pastel blue, and the ramp made the building feel round. The whole place felt like we were inside a toilet cleaner bottle. Every angle was the same color blue and the edges all curved together. I remember I couldn't walk very far.

By the time Mom lugged our suitcases, a sick child, and a 6-year-old social butterfly to a water fountain, she must have wanted to give up. Mom's hand was sweaty, and the aspirin had turned to mush in her hand.

We didn't have any other medicine and we were going to miss our train if we didn't hurry so, against my weak protests, I licked the aspirin from Mom's hand.

Thanks to the kindness of a few strangers who helped Mom with our bags, we made it onto the train headed for South Dakota just in the nick of time.

As we settled into our seats, Mom adjusted me on her lap and whispered in my ear. "They won't let us stay on the train if they know you're sick. Just stay wrapped up in the blanket on my lap and everyone will think you're sleeping." That was an easy command to obey.

I pretended to be sleeping when the man came by to check our tickets. He moved along to other passengers without suspicion. The next thing I knew, the train was chugging forward. The rhythmic sound of the train's chug-chug-chug along the tracks rocked me to sleep in my mother's arms.

I don't remember much about the train ride except Diane jumping and running up and down the aisle that ran between the seats of passengers. She bounded around the moving train and even went to other train cars all by herself. Diane told the other passengers how she was all by herself because her little sister was so sick, and many of them gave her quarters!

As Diane made friends with everyone on the passenger train, I slept on and off in Mom's arms. At times Mom tried to put me in Diane's seat, but it never lasted. However long that train ride was, Mom spent it anchored in place by a sick kid as the train chugged through the mountains.

When we reached our destination, it was obvious I had the mumps.

And no one had given me a single quarter.

There was no way I could go to my aunt's wedding, but all my relatives on Mom's side would be at the church. The only person left to watch me was Grandma Naomi. She was all smiles and happy talk when she walked through the front door of the Olson's farmhouse. She greeted the other side of my family as if she liked them. Meanwhile, I was lying on Grandma Mabel's couch, wrapped in a quilt. I could hear all their conversations, but the cheery woman with Grandma Naomi's voice wasn't anyone I knew. Whoever was in the kitchen with my mom was just a made-up person who would disappear as soon as no one was watching. After a few minutes of small talk, Grandma Naomi came over to the couch where I was lying.

The cheery woman from the kitchen disappeared and the mean woman I'd known all my life glared down at me. Even if no one else could see it, she clearly didn't want to be there.

She asked if there was anything I wanted.

"Could you read me my book?" I asked.

I only had one book that was really mine. It was the "Dr. Seuss Sleep Book" and I knew it by heart.

Grandma picked it up, balanced her reading glasses at the very tip of her nose, and crinkled her mouth into a scowl as she flipped through the pages. When she saw how many words were on each page, she told me we would save it for later.

After everyone was dressed in their beautiful gowns with perfect hair and makeup, they left me alone with Grandma Naomi. She wasn't one to put her hand on my forehead to relieve my fever headache, or even bring a cool washcloth to do the job. She was the grandmother who hated the idea of even touching me unless she had a soapy washcloth in hand to protect herself from "that filthy kid." Aka, me.

Grandma read the newspapers she'd brought along. She turned the channel on the television over and over as if more than the three television stations that existed would somehow appear. Finally, when there was nothing else for her to do, she agreed to read me the cherished book I had brought from Montana.

Mom read it to me every night at home. I loved to hear the way different voices sounded and how the words and phrases made nonsense come to life. Mom was a master at pronunciation and cadence. The rhymes and timings were perfect and simple when you pronounced the words correctly. Most people get that about Dr. Seuss, but Grandma Naomi wasn't most people. She found it irritating that the author made up words, and she didn't know how to pronounce anything.

After I'd corrected her mispronunciation of words five or six times, she started skipping pages. I thought it would be helpful if I let her know she'd missed an entire page in a story made of glorious words and imaginary creatures.

She did not find it helpful.

The second time I reminded her she had skipped pages, she slammed the book shut and said we were done. Grandma took my book and put it up on a counter. I couldn't reach it even if I'd been well enough to get off the couch. My vision blurred with tears as I stared at the book I loved, tormentingly close but impossibly out of reach. She didn't have to read it to me. I would have been very happy to lie nestled in the quilt, reading my book by myself. But no. That would have made me happy, and Grandma was having none of that. She told me I needed to get some sleep and went back to turning the knobs on the television.

When my family came home from the wedding, the house exploded with excitement and energy. My sister bounced up to me in her beautiful dress and twirled around, as I imagined she had done at the wedding dance.

I was supposed to wear a beautiful dress too.

Then Diane showed me the most amazing thing I'd ever seen: a beautiful rose made of frosting. I'd never seen anything so perfect in my life and it was like candy! More importantly, my sister had thought of me at the wedding and brought me a treat so I wouldn't miss out.

I'd always believed Diane just thought of me as a pain in the butt. I thought back to her protests when she wanted to play with her friends.

"Can I go to the park?" Diane would ask.

"Only if you take your sister along," was the only answer Diane ever received.

The only times she ever shared her feelings about me were when she yelled things like, "I hate you!" in the middle of one of our fights.

And yet now she was thinking about me and wishing I had been at the wedding to see the beautiful things she had seen. My heart warmed even beyond my fever. As I reached out my hand for the rose, Diane popped it into her mouth and chortled, "I got to eat these all night!" Then she skipped back into the kitchen where everyone who didn't want to be around a contagious kid was gathered. Everyone except Mom.

Mom walked up to the couch as my sister skipped out. A single tear ran down my cheek and the water felt like it was burning my skin. I turned my head into my pillow so Mom wouldn't see my tears. She sat down next to me on the couch like I wasn't even infectious and put her hand against my forehead. It never mattered how sick I was or even what was wrong with me, the feel of Mom's hand on my forehead made everything better.

I suppose I made us miss the train while I recovered, or maybe we only had one-way tickets. Whatever the reason, we didn't ride the train back to Montana. Instead, Grandpa Olson drove Mom, Diane, me, and the new pet I had fallen in love with at the Olson farm. It was a tiny piglet named Porky that Grandpa had given to Mom.

It was 1970, and children were allowed to roam vehicles untethered, regardless of their age. I spent the drive home holding my newest friend or snuggled next to him in a box on the floor of the back seat.

It was the best car ride ever! Who needed candy roses when I had my very own baby pig?

STOLEN UNDERPANTS

Our family of four became a family of five when Porky moved in. I don't know if he was supposed to be a gift of pork rather than a pet, but to me Porky was part of the family. He lived in our basement and absolutely loved scalloped potatoes. Unfortunately … he was a pig.

The basement floor was cement, so it wasn't a big deal when Porky made messes. Of course, I wasn't the one who had to clean up after him, so I can't really say how big of a deal it was. I do know it became significantly more difficult when Porky learned to climb the stairs. He rubbed his snout, filled with both slobber and scalloped potatoes on the edge of each step, leaving behind big old smears of snotty scalloped potatoes on the edge of every step.

I wasn't looking at the stairs when I came skipping down to talk to Mom. She was doing laundry as Porky watched from behind her. Halfway down the stairs I slipped in Porky's slime and landed on the cement floor. Once again, my arm was broken.

I don't remember it hurting. I don't even remember going to the hospital. But I do remember they wouldn't let me go home. The nurses made me put on a nightgown that tied in the back and hung down way below my feet. Then they took my underpants! I was mortified. I never … never went to bed without my underpants! Even with the sheet they draped over me, it still felt like I was breaking my treaty with the monsters under the bed. I felt like I was completely exposed and dirty. To top it all off, they didn't have a bed small enough for me, so they made me sleep in a crib! If something was coming to get me, there would be no way for me to get out of the crib without help. It didn't matter how much I cried. The crib wasn't optional.

They wheeled my crib into a big open room filled with two rows of single beds. In all, there were about twenty beds in the ward. All but a couple contained patients, but I was the only child. I was scared, but Mom was talking to me and holding onto the side of the crib, so everything would be okay. I hadn't even started to become sleepy when the nurse came in and told Mom she would have to leave. Visiting hours were over.

My mother was going to leave!

Having an older sibling, I had never in my life slept away from home by myself, or with strangers. I begged and pleaded, but the nurses were adamant. Mom could not stay.

Mom leaned over the bars of the crib and asked if there was anything I needed her to bring in the morning. All I could think of asking for was my underpants.

"Don't worry, I won't forget," Mom assured me before leaving me all by myself in a big room filled with sick people.

It was dark in the hospital ward, but they parked my crib near the doorway. Light from the nurses' station illuminated the area around my crib, but that only made it difficult to see what the patients in the back of the room were doing. What I couldn't see I could hear. There were deep phlegmy coughs and a chorus of moans. Some snored in their beds. All mixed together it sounded just like the monsters under the bed had all sprung to life.

I pulled the sheet up over my head and tucked it around my feet. Only my eyes remained uncovered as I stared through the bars of my prison. I wondered if the monsters could see me.

After what seemed like hours of watching each bed alternately, one of the groaners from the back of the ward sat up. From the sound of his wheezing, groaning, and coughing it sounded like that took a lot of effort. Eventually he rose to his feet. His slippers shuffled across the floor in a "thump, scratch" sound as he dragged his second foot behind just enough to make the scratching sound. He was coming toward my bed.

I had no idea what was wrong with him, and I only knew how to count to ten. I ran out of numbers, but the sounds continued—*thump, scraaaaatch, thump, scraaaaatch*. As his shadow formed on the wall, I could see he was a very skinny man, but the shadow stretched him out to a hundred feet tall. He was wearing the exact same nightie I'd been given.

He shuffled closer to my crib.

I carefully pulled the sheet tighter around my head. There were no hiding places inside the crib, so I pulled the pillow over my head and allowed just a small slit to see through. Lying as still as I could and breathing only when absolutely necessary, I watched the old man's movements. When the "scratch, thump man" was close enough, he was going to get me!

As he inched closer, I thought about screaming; but if he hadn't seen me, I'd just be giving away my hiding place. I held my breath.

The sheet that was making me invisible also blocked my view of the nurses' station. Would any of the people that told Mom they'd watch me still be there when he took the last step and grabbed me? Would they hear me scream?

By the time the skinny man reached my crib, I was sure he could hear my heart beating ridiculously loudly, as if it wanted the old man to get me. He put his hand on the bars by my feet, and my heart stopped.

Then he turned to take his next step toward the nursing station.

The next thing I knew Mom was saying it was time to wake up. I woke to her face leaning over the crib.

"Did you bring my underpants? I asked.

She had.

STICKS AND STONES AND MORE BROKEN BONES

Another six weeks in an itchy cast, and a new sling with animals on it. In the end, it turned out the doctor had been wrong. A person CAN break a bone in the exact same place more than once.

By the summer of my fourth year, the cast was off my arm, and I was trying, once again, to be a regular kid. The neighborhood children still flocked to our porch, in hopes my sister might come out to play. Even though they never invited me to play with them, they couldn't stop me from watching.

There was a wooden ledge all around our porch that was about six inches wide. One of the favorite games for neighborhood kids was to walk to the ledge and pretend it was a pirate's plank. One day there was an old couch thrown out in our yard ... right under the porch ledge. Finally, the neighborhood kids could literally force each other to walk the dreaded plank—and on over the edge. They giggled with delight as they landed on the old couch and bounced off onto their feet.

I wanted to join them, but I knew it would probably mean I'd end up in another cast and I didn't want that.

Voices rang out through the neighborhood as mothers called their children home. As the last of the kids ran out of the yard, Diane came out the front door.

"What were they doing?" she asked.

"Walking the plank," I answered.

"Jumping onto the couch?" She peered over the edge at the five-foot drop to the ground.

"Nope," I answered confidently. "They were jumping right onto the ground."

Knowing my sister's competitive nature, I giggled inside at the idea of getting revenge against my sister for the ice slide incident.

Diane jumped onto the porch ledge.

Oh, how I wished I were big enough to get up onto the porch ledge like the other kids! I wouldn't jump off, but oh, what an adventure it would be to walk the plank.

Diane reached the edge of the porch and turned to me to see if I was trying to pull one over on her. I remained stoic.

"Hey, you don't have to do it," I said, "but some of those kids were like three years old."

At that prompting, my sister soared off the edge of the ledge.

I was holding my stomach and laughing harder than I'd ever laughed in my life when my sister hit the ground.

"They were jumping onto the couch!" I cackled as I peered over the edge to see my sister lying on the ground. I was still laughing and pointing when my sister let out the first wail of pain. Both Mom and dad came running outside to see what was happening, and I immediately knew I was dead.

Dad ran into the apartment for just a second, then came running back with a blanket and keys. Mom wrapped the blanket around Diane and scooped her up into her arms.

"Get in the car!" Mom yelled to me as dad opened the passenger door of our station wagon so Mom could get in the front seat with Diane.

I was frozen on the porch. Eventually, they were going to figure out how Diane broke her leg, and I was going to be dead. The last thing in the world I wanted to do was get into that car.

"Hurry up!" Mom commanded from passenger side of the front seat while Diane screamed bloody murder from Mom's lap.

My body thawed and I ran to the driver's side of the car. The doors were too heavy for me to open myself, so dad opened the door, and I climbed inside. Dad sped off so quickly I flew back against the seat.

My sister's leg was broken, and her cast was huge. It covered her leg from toes to hip, and the neighborhood kids argued over whose turn it was to pull Diane around in her wagon. By the time it was removed, her cast was covered with signatures and well wishes smeared from the heat of summer. No one ever signed my casts; but in fairness, none of my friends knew how to write yet.

That was what school was for, after all.

***

On my first day of kindergarten, I sat at my L-shaped desk in my best dress. It was 1971 and girls were required to wear dresses to school. The classroom was decorated with colored letters and so many toys! The biggest thing though—the item I could not wait to play with—was a child-sized kitchen with a refrigerator, sink, stove, the whole shebang! I had never seen anything like it, and I was itching in my seat to explore the room.

As the teacher called roll, students yelled out "here" or "present" when they heard their name. I was gazing around the room, lost in my own world, when the teacher read a name and silence followed. After a few seconds my attention perked, and I turned to the teacher. She read the name again.

Looking around the room again, I was focused on my fellow students rather than the toys. Who was so stupid they didn't know their own name? After silence followed the third reading of that strange name, the teacher came up to my desk.

"Isn't that you?" she asked me.

"No," I replied politely, "I'm Scooter."

"No, you're not." She proceeded to tell me my new name, a stupid name I had never heard before in my entire life. Then she wrote it on a slip of paper and taped it to my desk. From that moment forward, I would have to be "Colleen," whether I liked it or not—even if she did spell it incorrectly.

Apparently, the name change bothered me enough that Mom went to the school to ask them to call me Scooter, but the teacher wouldn't hear of it.

While my sister was a celebrity on her crutches, I did my best to just blend in. At the end of the day when we would meet to walk home, she would be surrounded by a group of admirers who wanted to help hold her books or help put her boots on. More than anything, I wished I were like my sister.

***

School may have been traumatic, but at the end of the day and on weekends, I had my best friends.

Missy's parents played in other bands as well as dad's, so they weren't always around while we lived in Montana. When they were gone, I had my best friend Denise, who lived upstairs.

Neither Denise nor I were able to cross streets, but there were tons of things to explore in our neighborhood, and that was exactly what we did. One of our favorite activities was to crawl inside the dumpster behind our apartment and search for treasures. One day we found the greatest treasure of all time: a full box of name-brand cereal that was filled with tiny colorful marshmallows.

Denise's family couldn't afford name-brand foods any more than my family could, but we felt like the most spoiled kids in the world. We could throw the healthy parts of the cereal all around us and focus exclusively on the marshmallows. In that moment we were royalty who could cast aside our trash for others to pick up, even if it was only in our imaginations.

No one ever missed us during our explorations; but if a child's scream ever rang out, mothers swarmed out of doors like bees leaving their hives. One day we found out just how fast our mothers could run.

Denise and I had learned about making doll heads from dried apples and couldn't wait to make our own. With apples in hand, we went to the steps of our big porch and set our apples in the sunniest spot we could find. Then we waited.

We waited until the sun moved away from our apples, then moved them onto the sidewalk to keep them in sunlight. We watched our apples intently. The last thing we wanted to do was miss the moment our apples shriveled into doll heads.

That's when Perry came by to visit. Perry was a neighborhood boy the same age as Denise and me who never missed an opportunity to annoy us. On this day, Perry had his cap gun and extra rolls of caps, so he came up to the porch with his gun blazing.

"Leave us alone," Denise ordered. "We're making dolls."

"No, you're not," Perry replied. "You're dead."

Bang, bang, bang, rang out as Perry just kept getting closer and closer. Finally, he was shooting his cap gun right in our ears.

That was the moment Denise had enough. She grabbed Perry's cap gun from his hand and cracked him over the head with it as hard as she could.

Perry's eyes widened in slow motion as it dawned on him that he had been hit.

A drip of blood ran out of Perry's hairline and down his forehead. Feeling the drip, he put his hand to his forehead and pulled it back to see red.

Perry went insane.

He started screaming and crying and hollering "I've been shot!" at the top of his lungs. Mothers poured out of doors from every direction to see whose child was screaming. Denise's mom and my mom had both been inside our apartments, so they were coming down the porch steps within seconds. Perry's mom was running across the street screaming his name as she ran.

"What happened?" Mom asked as she rushed to check Perry's wound. I shrugged my answer just as Perry's mom came upon us and asked the same question.

"She hit me!" Perry screamed. "Denise hit me with my gun! I think she shot me!"

Perry's mother snatched him off the ground and ran back to their house.

Meanwhile at our house, the moms still expected answers.

Denise and I babbled our versions of the story to our respective mothers. As we incoherently told the tale of our mission to make shrunken-apple doll heads, our exasperated mothers pulled us by the arms into our own apartments.

"What were you thinking?" Mom asked as she closed our apartment door to the outside world.

"I didn't … hit him! I was just … waiting for my apple to shrink … so I could make a doll," I sobbed as I finally had the chance to explain to my mother what happened.

"That takes several days in bright hot sunlight," Mom explained. "And the apple has to be peeled."

I was still sent to bed, but when allowed to come out of my room, Mom peeled my apple and helped me find a place for it in our yard. Of course, I lost interest in it long before the apple ever turned into anything resembling a wrinkled face.

***

When the leaves on the trees began to change color, my parents made the announcement we'd heard so many times before: "We are moving."

Diane's broken leg had just healed, and she was more popular than ever. But three- and six-year-olds don't have a say about the sticks and stones that are cast upon them.

SING DAMMIT OR YOU'RE GOING TO BED WITH THE MONSTERS

Mom went through the all-too-familiar routine of moving. Step one meant driving to grocery stores and asking them for chicken boxes. They were the best boxes for moving because they had lids. Step two was packing everything we owned, which didn't take long since we had very little. Lastly, Mom loaded our lives into the station wagon and waited for dad to give the command to leave.

As we drove away from the mountains, all Diane and I knew was that we would be living in South Dakota. Since both sets of grandparents and even our great-grandmother lived where we would be moving, it didn't seem scary. Plus, my best friend and her family were following closely behind in their bus house.

Living closer to Grandma and Grandpa Olson was wonderful but living closer to Grandma Naomi meant having to see her more often too.

I hated that.

From what I've been told, my father's mother and I didn't see eye-to-eye from day one. As a newborn baby, when Grandma Naomi picked me up, I would hold my breath until I turned blue.

I suppose I can't really fault her for disliking me in return.

For the most part I just tried to stay out of her sight. That approach seemed to work great for her as well. Unless, of course, she wanted my sister and me to sing.

In those early days, dad almost always had his band equipment in the back of our station wagon. Every so often Grandma would convince him to set some of it up in her living room. Usually that meant a microphone stand, complete with a microphone that wasn't plugged into anything, a personal amplifier, and dad's guitar. The microphone stand was always set up in front of Grandma's console television.

"Did you touch buttons on here?"

She asked the question every single time she turned on the television part of her console. "Well, somebody's been touching it. The color's all screwed up again. Jesus, Mary, and Joseph, can't you be around anything without messing it up?"

Of course, the television wasn't necessary for the live shows she expected my sister and me to perform on her command.

Her living room was longer than it was wide, and every seat pointed directly at the television. Once the equipment was set up, Grandma would make her requests.

"How about something from Johnny Cash?" she would yell from across the room as if she were in a crowded nightclub.

"We don't know any Johnny Cash," my sister or I would answer.

"What about Elvis? You certainly must know an Elvis song, for God's sake." Irritation rang in her voice.

"We can sing it to a record." Our answers always sounded more like questions by that point. It didn't matter that there was a twenty-foot-wide record player sitting inside the top compartment of her console television. For some reason, singing along with records was never an option.

"Jesus, Mary, and Joseph! I'm not going to go all the way over there and dig through the records," Grandma would complain. "Then I've got to switch the console over from TV to stereo. The TV's just starting to work again after you kids messed with the knobs last time. Just sing whatever song you know."

By this point in the evening, neither my sister nor I ever felt much like singing. Besides completely blanking on any songs we knew, the pressure to perform up to her expectations became scarier and scarier. This was usually around the time one of us tried to back out.

"I don't want to sing anymore."

"Oh, come on now. You have a beautiful voice. Sing something." Grandma would lighten her tone just a bit at the first protest.

"I don't feel like it," I would say quietly, looking down.

By that point I worried I might vomit on Grandma's new shag carpet. Grandma's carpet wasn't just important to her because it was new. It was a status symbol, and she made sure it always had perfectly measured rake marks across it. Yes, she had a special rake for her shag carpeting.

As I studied the carpet, Grandma's frustration grew.

"Sing dammit or you're going to bed!"

And that was always the introduction for our living room concert of "I'm Henry the Eighth I Am," from Herman's Hermits.

It was the only song we knew by heart so Grandma would have us do at least two rounds.

When my sister and I were finally allowed to leave the "stage," Grandma would reveal her ulterior motive. It was time for dad to sing. I don't know if he needed an opening act, time to drink a couple of "highballs," or just lowered expectations, but it never took long for her to convince him to "Just do a couple of my favorites."

It was fun to watch dad when he was that person. He would close his eyes during the parts of the song that were sad, and he laughed at things that were funny. He was the guy everyone in our world loved.

It was difficult for me to understand the flip-flops in his personality, but Grandma Naomi was always consistent. She adored my father, loved my sister, tolerated my mother, and detested me.

***

During those early years, Mom tried to leave dad several times. Grandpa Olson disliked my father from the beginning, so when Mom decided to marry him, Grandpa said, "Then don't ever ask me for any help or support."

She never did. In fact, my older sister was a year old before Grandpa finally swallowed his pride and visited. Even then, it was only because he had to go into the hospital and needed someone to watch my aunt.

Dad's parents were even less helpful. Every time Mom was ready to leave dad, his mother would say, "You would really leave him after everything we've done for you?" Then she'd bring up money they'd loaned my parents or free babysitting she'd provided. She'd even go so far as to use Christmas presents to guilt Mom into turning the other black-and-blued cheek.

At the end of the day, Mom had nowhere to go. No one was going to save her.

Her monster was already on top of the bed.

A MIRACULOUS TRANSFORMATION

Mom had left college to marry dad, and we never stayed in one place long enough for her to build a good work history. Even if those hadn't been issues, we only ever had one car. While those obstacles kept Mom from building a career, they never stopped her from working.

While dad played in the band, she convinced the bar manager to let her wait tables for tips. She worked hard, so the managers usually threw any extra work they could in her direction. Sometimes that meant bartending, sometimes it meant cleaning the bar the morning after. Whatever it was, Mom always did her best and excelled.

Mom's world consisted of 23½-hour workdays, but dad's world consisted of bars and parties. He and his friends were always laughing and joking and having a great time. It didn't matter what night of the week it was, someone was always available to go drinking.

Even as a small child I could never understand how Mom was able to get out of bed when dad and his friends came stumbling in at three in the morning. She cheerfully made the intruders breakfast in the middle of the night and still awakened Diane and me in time for school.

***

Our new abode was a trailer house that looked like pictures of blimps I had seen. It was rounded on both ends and entirely silver. I marveled at the way the silver shone in the bright sunlight. What I didn't know was that glistening sparkle from the outside heated the inside to about a hundred and fifty degrees. The first time I remember Mom complaining was during the summer of 1972.

She was eight months pregnant when we first pulled up to the silver bullet house. There was a small gravel parking spot in front of the trailer and a tiny patch of grass behind where my sister and I could play. Toward the back of each trailer house the yard became much larger as it blended into the neighboring trailer's yard. This is where I met our neighbor for the first time.

I don't remember the woman's name, but the first time we met she was busy hanging freshly washed clothes on her clothesline.

"When is your baby due?" I asked, but it was more of an opening for me to tell her I was going to have a new baby in the house any day.

The woman stared at me for a couple of seconds. "I'm not pregnant," she replied.

Her big round stomach poked out just as far as Mom's did. I wondered how in the world she could be that close to having a baby and not know it.

"Yes, you are," I argued.

"No, I'm not," she replied with much more enunciation than she had used in her previous answer. I knew what that meant.

"Okay," I replied even though I still wasn't convinced. "See you later."

I walked back to my own yard and straight up the two metal steps of our trailer house. Mom was sitting at the "dining room" table drinking a cup of coffee when I came in mumbling my frustration to myself.

"What's the matter?" Mom asked.

"That lady next door said she's not pregnant," I answered indignantly.

"She's not!" Mom barely finished her answer before she bolted out the door, and that's how my mom became friends with our new neighbor.

I don't know if moving closer to his parents made dad take his responsibilities more seriously or if Mom had given him an ultimatum, but it wasn't long after we moved back to South Dakota that dad took a job driving truck. It was the first "real" job I'd ever known my father to have, and I was more than a little impressed when he showed us the truck he drove.

The truck wasn't just big—it was the biggest vehicle I'd ever seen in my whole entire life, and that included Grandpa Olson's tractor! Behind the driver and passenger seats was a full-sized bed that dad used during long hauls. On the rare occasions he took all of us along with him, it was where Diane and I rode. Seat belts weren't any more of a thing in semi-trucks than they were in our station wagon, so Diane and I were free to play or sleep or whatever we wanted. It even had its own light!

On one trip, Diane and I were supposed to be going to sleep, but neither of us was tired. As soon as Mom told us goodnight and pulled the curtain to close us in, Diane reached up and pulled the chain that clicked on our light.

It wasn't half a second before we heard, "Turn that light off!"

How could they know?

Diane obediently pulled the chain to toggle the light back off, then lay back down on the mattress.

"Do you think she heard me turn on the light?" Diane asked.

"Probably," I answered.

"Ok, so when I pull the switch, you cough or something to make a bunch of noise," she instructed.

"Okay." By the light of passing traffic, I eagerly watched for my sister to pull the chain.

No matter how hard I tried, I could never master the timing of my cough. Inevitably, Mom opened the curtain immediately after the light came on every time we tried. Eventually the game itself would make Diane and me tired enough to fall asleep.

I don't know what company my father drove for, or even what he was carrying, but I will never forget the amazing lights illuminating every inch of our destination. Millions of bulbs sparkled and shone on tall silver buildings that I now know were grain elevators. To me, it looked like we had landed amongst the stars themselves. I closed my eyes to wish on all the twinkling lights at once. "Twinkle, twinkle little star, I hope our lives are always like this."

By the time Mom was nine months pregnant and the temperatures were consistently reaching over one hundred degrees, the rides in dad's truck were over. He, however, continued to be gone several days each week.

I wish I could say Diane and I did everything we could to make the final days of Mom's pregnancy easier for her, but we were too busy laughing at her.

Shortly before Mom went into labor the doctor discovered the baby was breech. The doctor's solution was that she needed to stand on her head against a wall—or at least try— several times each day. Most of the time she laughed right along with us as she tried to thrust herself upside down and backwards against a corner of our tiny trailer.

She never really accomplished a headstand, but the efforts did turn the baby. For the first time in my life, I was about to become a big sister, and I couldn't wait! I was overjoyed when Grandma and Grandpa Olson showed up to take us out to their farm because

Mom was going into the hospital. I couldn't have been prouder as I stood in the hospital parking lot and looked up at the third-floor window where Mom held our brand-new baby brother. Hospitals didn't allow filthy kids to visit in 1972.

Part of me believed dad might be different after he had a son. For a while he even was. But it didn't last.

I, however, was eternally transformed when my baby brother came into the world.

CIGARETTES AND CHEWING GUM

I was only six-and-a-half years old when Mom walked through our door carrying a blanket containing my baby brother Mark. My bones wanted to jump out of my skin at the idea of holding the tiny human Mom peeled the blanket back to reveal.

I'd had dolls for as long as I could remember, but Mark was different. He was alive! He moved, so I wasn't allowed to hold him unless I was sitting in a chair with arms. My nervous excitement—and the fact that I'd already broken three bones—likely gave Mom zero confidence in my abilities, but I didn't care what the rules were. If I had been required to run five miles before I was able to hold him, I would have run five miles. I adored my baby brother … everyone did!

His head was completely bald, but I endlessly petted any fuzz that started to sprout. His head was just so perfectly round, like Charlie Brown's. His huge blue eyes followed every move Diane or I made, and we were both fiercely protective from the second he came into our world. Nothing had messed him up yet and he looked at everyone with those big blue eyes filled with wonder and delight.

When he looked at me, it seemed like he was saying "*I trust you*," even though he had no reason to believe I was trustworthy. I swore a promise the moment I saw him: no matter what happened, I would always protect him. My baby brother became both the driving force and the recipient of my advocacy. People could do whatever they wanted to me, but no one would ever hurt my baby brother … not if I was alive.

In addition to having an extra mouth to feed, Mom and dad had hospital bills that needed to be paid. When the money Mom brought in didn't cover our bills and the money dad made didn't make it home, Mom took on another job. Even though we spent a lot of time with babysitters, I don't remember ever feeling like Mom wasn't there for us. She might not have been there when we went to sleep, but she was always there when we awoke. She was always there if we were scared in the middle of the night. And the babysitters were all part of the adventure.

One of them was a college student who told Mom she would just be studying "after the kids were asleep," so Mom could stay out as long as necessary. Perhaps that should have been a give-away, because that girl threw the biggest party I'd ever seen in my life. There must have been a million people in our tiny trailer house. Some of them were kissing, some of them were doing more than kissing. Almost all of them were moving to the loud music. Diane and I mingled amongst the crowd as people who seemed like adults to us offered us beer and cigarettes. I'd smoked my first cigarette at five years old when dad thought it would be funny to make me take a hit. I coughed and gagged, so I guess it didn't count as smoking a whole cigarette. That didn't happen until I was six.

In the morning, Mom asked us what had happened to the house, and we couldn't wait to tell her stories about the things we'd seen. The living room was covered in beer bottles; the ceiling had gum stuck on it, and there were burn marks in the carpet. Apparently, the neighbor had been complaining all morning about hooligans peeing in her yard. That complaint would wind up biting her in the butt because after that, when Mom was in a pinch, she sometimes did have to ask our neighbor—who never did have her baby, by the way—to watch us.

The woman was always outside screaming swear words at her kids, who were usually doing something naughty. It was her son who shot my sister in the back with a BB gun one summer afternoon. But that wasn't the only thing we disliked about her. The whole time she was at our house she just sat on the couch and ate whatever she could find in the cupboards while she watched TV.

We could do whatever we wanted, except disturb her. Unfortunately, the only thing there was to do was watch TV.

One night before the neighbor showed up to watch us, Mom pulled out a bag of potato chips and told us we could have them as a special treat while we watched a movie that was going to be on television that night. Potato chips were a rare splurge in our household, so the fact that we were going to get to eat them while watching a movie was the most exciting surprise I could imagine. I couldn't wait until seven o'clock when I would sit on the couch with my sister, each with our own bowl of chips, watching TV. It was all I could think about, and I asked the babysitter repeatedly if it was time for the movie.

The neighbor lady did let us watch the movie, and as it started, I asked if we could have our chips. She said no but she didn't give me a reason. I figured that meant we were going to wait until the first commercial. A little while into the movie, I asked again if we could have our snack and reminded her that Mom said we could.

She'd heard enough out of me and sent me to bed: no movie and no chips.

I hated the fact that adults always won no matter what, but since she weighed about 400 pounds that wouldn't be a battle I could win. Most likely she'd just break me in half. If compared to a celebrity, my closest look-alike would have been Olive Oyle.

It wasn't just that I looked sickly; I was sickly. In addition to my fragile bones, I always seemed to get viruses worse than normal people. The chicken pox left thousands of blistered sores all around my body—in my nose, my mouth, my eyelids. I'd caught them from Diane who had four or five pox.

I caught everything.

The fact that I wasn't as healthy as other kids gave my dad and his mother one more reason to hate me.

Grandma Naomi never missed an opportunity to tell me what a "filthy" kid I was. She even had special bed sheets for when my siblings and I spent the night. As far as I knew, we were the only people who ever slept in their spare bedroom, but that didn't matter. The nighttime routine always involved stripping the sheets that were on the bed and replacing them with different ones that my sister and I were allowed to sleep in. We didn't have accidents, but she wasn't taking any chances with exposure to our germs.

In addition to special sheets, there was bedtime scrubbing. Grandma ran the faucet in her bathroom until steam rose from the water coming out. She then took one of her pure white terry cloth washcloths and held it under the water until it was completely saturated.

The rag was scalding when she put it against my skin and abrasive as she scrubbed my filth away. After aggressively wiping my neck, she always held the washcloth in front of my face to show all the filth she had removed. With a face as red as a baboon's ass and a neck raw from involuntary exfoliation, I would climb into one of the twin beds that had belonged to my dad and his younger brother David.

Regardless of Grandma's efforts to sterilize my body, I still caught everything. One night at our house during a particularly bad respiratory infection, I couldn't stop coughing. I knew how hard Mom worked and I didn't want to disturb her sleep, but I just couldn't keep the coughs inside. I tried lying on my stomach and coughing into my pillow. I tried pulling the blanket over the back of my head while I coughed into the pillow, but nothing could completely muffle the sounds.

Mom slipped out of bed and walked across the house. I deserved to get in trouble for keeping her awake when she was hardly ever able to sleep. It would have made sense if she was mad, but that wasn't who my mother was. She sat down on my bed and put her palm against my forehead.

Better.

Mom rubbed my back to help ease the muscles that were clenched in spasms from my coughing. She patted my back to help whatever was stuck in my lungs come up, and she stayed with me until I fell asleep. It didn't matter what it was that was wrong, Mom could make everything better.

I wanted so badly to be big and strong and able to protect my mom, but I knew I wouldn't ever be physically strong enough to do that. I could, however, protect my baby brother, even if it did have to be while I was sitting down.

As my brother grew bigger he remained my favorite hobby, but he also became Mom's. The extra draw on her time meant Diane and I were given extra freedom. One of the best things about our trailer court was that it sat right next to the city zoo where, at six years old, I would accept my first job.

UGLY FEATHERS AND DANDELIONS

On Saturdays when it was nice, Diane would ask if she could ride her bike to the zoo. Mom's answer was always the same: "If you take your sister with you."

Diane hated having to take me places, but she knew it was useless to put up a fight. She'd just have to suffer through it if she wanted to go. And she always did.

My sister's best friend lived on the opposite side of the zoo and spent as much time in the free playground as Diane and I did. It was a great place for kids because the entire zoo was free!

There was a driveway that stretched from one end of the zoo to the other. It was about the length of a football field, with sidewalks next to the animal pens on one side of the driveway and the parking lot/playground on the other side. There was a tall metal slide that rose higher than any of the surrounding buildings and burned your butt if you tried to go down it in the summer. There were swings that consisted of rubber strips connected to chains. Any weight at all made the rubber seat fold together and pinch both sides of my butt. I hated those swings, but it didn't matter. I wasn't there for the playground equipment. From the second I hopped off my bike, my one-track mind was focused on the animal cages.

"Hey, get away from that cage and come over here," my sister would beckon.

Since Diane and I usually arrived at the park first, she always made me sit with her at one of the picnic tables until her friend arrived. I loved those times when my sister had nothing to do but talk to me. I sometimes hoped there would be a day she and her friend would ask me to play with them, but once Miranda arrived, they jumped on their bikes and pedaled away as fast as they could, leaving me behind.

But I had things to do.

At first, I just stood up against the fences that kept people away from the animals. My long skinny arms could reach a fair distance inside the pen, but I still had to coax the animals to come close. I tried picking leaves and holding them out as far as I could into the fence. I spoke softly and reminded them repeatedly I would never hurt them. My goal was to lure them close enough that I could pet one of the animals. I didn't even care which animal, but some were easier to coax than others.

The white-tailed mule deer were the first to warm up to my friendship. After an hour or so of talking quietly to the one deer who was brave enough to trust my intentions, he let me pet his neck. After several weeks of doing the same thing, my deer friend would come to the fence as soon as he saw me approach.

One day when I walked up to the deer containment, I saw a man trying to feed my deer a cigarette butt.

Some idiot was using the trust I'd spent countless hours earning to hurt my friend. I was pissed! I ran up to the man and yelled at him to get the cigarette butt away from my deer.

The man turned my direction, looked down at me and sneered, "Tsk, stupid kid," but he walked away.

I tried reaching my arm through the fence to get the cigarette away from my deer, but he was suddenly scared of me. He had no way to understand why I was suddenly a person who yelled and reached in his fence like I wanted to grab him. I *did* want to grab him, but only to get the cigarette away from him. I tried my best to explain, but he was already backing away and my frantic explanation gave him no peace.

All I knew at that time was that the deer no longer wanted to be my friend. I spent the rest of my day trying to lure him back toward me, but he wanted nothing to do with me. With a heavy heart I turned my attention to the spider monkeys. They quickly became my favorite.

Since the monkeys were more dangerous than the deer, they had a second fence far outside their enclosure that kept me from getting within ten feet of their cage. No matter how hard I tried, there was no way for me to get in or reach my arm far enough to pet any of them ... not even when they reached back. I stopped trying to reach them when I found out they liked to throw their poop.

The only other animals in my zoo were the birds, and the prairie dogs that lived in their enclosure. I was positive the zoo had every kind of bird in the world. There were red ones and blue ones and purple ones with beautiful feathers that sometimes fell out. There were huge birds, tiny birds, and everything in between, and each of them dropped the occasional feather. Once again, it paid to have long skinny arms at a zoo.

The grandest prize was the peacock feather, but none of them were ever close enough to the fence for me to reach, even with my arm in all the way. The one thing I knew for sure was this: the prettier the feather, the harder the birds seemed to hold onto them.

After several Saturdays alone at the park, a man who worked there started talking to me. He had keys to everything and could go inside with every single kind of animal whenever he wanted. He asked if I wanted to help him take care of them and oh boy did I ever!

It was a dream job for me that included all the corn I could feed to the animals and any feathers I could find! Except the peacock feathers, of course. The zoo sold those in the gift shop. Picking feathers inside the fence was way different than reaching through the wire. For one thing, the birds stopped pecking at my fingers when I reached for feathers. Their confidence disappeared when there wasn't a fence holding me back.

I worked as hard as I could to do my job well. I was convinced my access to the animals depended on my ability to follow the rules, and I really, really wanted to pet a spider monkey.

Every opportunity I had I went to the zoo, ever optimistic that one day my worker friend would let me in with the monkeys.

One day he sat me down to talk to me, and I thought "This is it."

It wasn't.

Someone new was the boss of the zoo, and they didn't want any kids to be inside the areas with animals. At first I thought he meant I should guard against intruding youth. Then I realized he meant me.

My relationship with the animals went back to being separated by fences. I no longer had handfuls of corn to offer them. The new manager put in vending machines that required quarters to get animal feed. I didn't have any money. It wasn't that kind of job.

Some of the animals remembered and loved me anyway. Some of them had better things to do than spend time with someone who had nothing to offer. But every so often my worker friend would sneak me a peacock feather to take home for Mom.

Mom, who asked nothing for herself, always acted like the feathers were crown jewels. She fawned over each one, even if it had some crumpled parts where I held it too tightly in the wrong places.

"Now I just have to find the perfect place for it," Mom would say as she walked around the living room with her new feather. They always went into the same vase, but Mom's search somehow made the feathers seem that much more treasured.

Mom treasured everything, even the ugly feathers and dandelions, but I could tell from her smile the peacock feathers were her favorite. For the first time in my life, I felt like I added something valuable to my mother's life.

Maybe my existence wasn't the worst thing to ever happen to my family.

"WHITE PANTS PEOPLE"

One day when my sister's friend Miranda arrived at the park to meet us, she brought her little brother Jessy along. Jessy was already eight and instantly became my boyfriend.

Day after day when Diane and Jessy's sister abandoned us in the park, we played together, had picnics with any snacks our mothers sent along, and played on the life-threatening playground equipment.

It wasn't long before we ran out of ideas for things to do in the park. The day he asked me to go with him to his house to play games I was looking particularly beautiful. I was wearing my brand-new, pure white pants that Mom warned me not to soil with grass stains.

Jessy's house would be perfect! We could play inside, and I could pretend I was used to being a "White Pants Person."

There were lots of people in my world who were "White Pants People." Donna had been one. The model my father's friend brought home with him from Las Vegas wore white pants. They were the fancy people who didn't get dirty. Their hair was always perfectly done, the women's makeup was always professionally applied, and they always wore dress shoes. I didn't have any dress shoes, but my tennis shoes would be good enough. After all, it was my first day as a "White Pants person."

Even though I wasn't supposed to cross the road to Jessy's house by myself, he was older and crossed it all the time. Reassuring myself that Mom would say yes anyway, I agreed to go.

His house was as close to the zoo as my trailer park was but on the opposite side. I looked over my shoulder frequently to see if

Mom was screaming, "Scooter! Get back here!" but she never did. I was in the clear!

Jessy's house was like nothing I had ever seen. He had thirteen brothers and sisters, so their home was a big steel Quonset converted into a home. I couldn't wait to see the inside!

Milk companies still offered home delivery in those days, and as we approached his front door, it looked like they were opening a grocery store. There were eight gallons of milk sitting in two crates. They had to be rich!

Their kitchen/dining room table resembled the picnic tables from the park, but there were three pushed together to make room for everyone in the family. Everything in their home was simple but multiplied in quantities I could never imagine having in my own house.

Jessy's mother was washing dishes at the kitchen sink wearing an apron like ones I'd seen my Grandma Olson wear. I imagined Jessy's mom spent a lot of hours washing dishes at that sink.

The oldest kid was twenty-three and in college. He sat at the kitchen table doing homework as three little kids sat around him with plates of food in front of them.

The living room had no television, just a collage of couches and a big old radio. Everywhere you looked was another kid, but Jessy was taking me deeper into his home. Sooner or later, he had to run out of siblings.

I followed Jessy around a corner to a hidden stairway that led to a basement. We descended the bare wood stairs with no railing on either side, just a drop off that would lead to the single-most embarrassing moment of my life. Fortunately, I wasn't wearing the high heels that would have made me a true "White Pants Person."

"Do you like to play ping pong?" Jessy asked just as I noticed a big blue table with a small net across the center. I'd never heard of ping pong before, but the sound of his voice made two of his younger siblings chime in.

"We're first!" a child who came up to my chin said as he grabbed the paddle from Jessy's hands.

"We already called it." A boy who was taller than Jessy said loudly. Both of their voices rang out in the big open basement. Jessy wasn't kidding. That was the fun place in the house! They had Gnip Gnop, a checkers board, boxing robots, and nearly every other toy I'd ever seen a commercial for on TV.

We played games with his younger siblings and annoyed his older ones. I had no idea how to keep track of time, but I started to think Diane might be looking for me. Imagining the trouble I would be in if Mom found out I'd crossed the road increased my heart rate.

"We should go back to the zoo," I told Jessy just when it was our turn to play ping pong.

"No, they won't be back yet. It's only been a little while." He pulled my hand back as I started toward the stairs. "Let's just watch one cartoon and then we'll go."

He had hit on my weakness.

"Okay, but then we gotta go," I said.

Jessy led me to a couch across the basement that sat across from a very small television set. It was just a corner of the basement really, but it was set up in a way that offered privacy and comfort.

I immediately knew something was wrong the second my butt hit the cushion of the dark brown couch. My bottom slid in a way it shouldn't on upholstered furniture and the smell told me immediately what happened—I, on my first day as a "White Pants Person" had sat in cat poop.

Without thinking I stood up and reached around to feel my backside. Yup, it was poop, and now it was all over my hands too. My mouth fell open as I gaped at my hands, and I was positive I would die of embarrassment as I looked up to make eye contact with Jessy. I wasn't really a "White Pants Person," and he was going to find out.

Then it dawned on me ... Mom! My mom was going to find out I had been to Jessy's house when she saw the poop on my pants. She would know I crossed the road and she would never let me go to the zoo again.

"It's okay ... Mom!" Jessy hollered. "It's okay ... Mom!!"

"What is it?" Jessy's mom answered down the stairs.

"Come down here quick! Scooter sat in poop!" His frantic declaration of my problem only increased my embarrassment.

"Bring her up here and I'll take care of it." His mother's calm reply to our problem was a clear indication it would take more than just poopy pants to phase the mother of fourteen kids.

She did her best to wipe my pants off with a wet rag, but I wasn't willing to take my pants off in front of my boyfriend, so when I left their house, I still had a large brown stain on the butt of my new white pants.

As I walked back across the road alone, pre-occupied with ideas of what Mom was going to do to me when she saw my pants, I watched for my sister. She wasn't there yet, which meant I would have too much time to spend lost in my own head.

Grass stains! Even if I couldn't get rid of the poop stain, I could certainly cover it up! Excited for the first time since Jessy's basement, I dropped down on my butt and began scooting around the grass. By the time Diane arrived, I was completely convinced I had camouflaged my problem with enough terrain to cover any remnants of cat poop.

Mom's bionic sense of smell kicked in the second Diane and I walked through the door of our trailer house.

"Oh my God, which one of you stepped in cat poop?" Mom asked as she rushed toward us to check the shoes we were taking off.

"It's me," I answered so quietly it was almost a whisper. I was busted. Mom would know I crossed the road. "I sat in cat poop at Jessy's house, but I didn't ride my bike on the street and he's a lot older than I am. We watched for cars really close and there weren't any coming either way," I was still blathering my excuses when Mom interrupted.

"Just go change your clothes." Mom covered her nose and turned her head away from me. "You stink."

Surprised that I didn't get into any trouble at all, I walked to the room I shared with my sister and changed into clean clothes.

It wouldn't occur to me until decades later that I could have just said I sat in animal poop at the park, but such is life.

I walked back to the kitchen where my mom was standing at the sink. She took the soiled slacks from my hands and put them into the sink to hand scrub the stains.

"Some people just aren't 'White Pants People,'" Mom said.

But I really, really wanted to be.

SURPRISE DEFENDER

While it didn't seem like I was going to get in trouble for crossing the road without permission, I did, in fact receive my first grounding that day. My family was going on a camping/hunting trip in only a few days. Did being grounded mean I would have to stay home all by myself?

When I asked Mom, she just said, "We'll have to see."

With nothing to do but ponder how I would take care of myself if everyone else was gone, I started getting used to the idea of being alone. I was confident I knew how to make toast, and I could always eat cereal. The milk jug was super heavy to lift, but I was sure I could do it if necessary.

As I thought about my independence, Mom stood at the sink washing my white pants and Mark's dirty diapers. Disposable diapers had recently become available, but they were expensive. Unless Mom received some as a gift, she used cloth diapers and rubber pants on my baby brother. I remember the deep impressions from the elastic around his chubby little legs any time the rubber pants came off.

My thoughts were interrupted by Mark's screams from the back of the trailer. He was awake, and Mom scurried through the hallway to tend to his needs.

After she disappeared into the back, I noticed she'd left her cigarettes and matches on the kitchen counter. Almost every adult from my childhood smoked, so there were always cigarettes lying around somewhere, but my thoughts of independence that day made me take special notice.

I crept to the kitchen from my seat on the couch and walked to the counter. Keeping my eyes on the far bedroom door down the hallway, I reached up and slid a cigarette out of Mom's pack. There still being no sign of her, I grabbed the matches and ran outside.

My grounding didn't include our yard, and Mom was busy with my baby brother, so I snuck behind our trailer and looked around. No one was in sight. It took me a few tries to get the match lit, but once I had a flame, I lit the cigarette and took a deep drag. My lungs burned at the intrusion of smoke, and I immediately started coughing. By the time I had my coughing fit under control and was ready to take a second drag, I heard the front door of our trailer open.

Thinking quickly, I threw the lit cigarette into a pile of leaves and debris that had collected directly behind the trailer. Hidden! And just in time.

Mom came around the corner of the house and saw me.

"What are you doing?" she asked.

"Nothing," I brilliantly retorted as I stole a glance in the direction of my discarded cigarette. It was then that I noticed a thin ghost of smoke rising from the leaves.

"Let's go back inside." I started to grab Mom's hand to skip away when she noticed the plume of smoke. It had grown much thicker, and a small orange flame was trying to lick every dry leaf around it.

I was busted.

Mom stomped out the fire before it could spread too far. Now I was double grounded. This time I was positive I would be left home alone; but for the immediate future I was sent to my room.

As it turned out, they did not leave me home alone.

The trip itself wasn't memorable and has blended into every other hunting trip we took during my childhood, but our return home was something I'll never forget.

As dad pulled the station wagon into our gravel parking spot, my bicycle was not where I'd left it. I remembered specifically, because I hadn't been able to ride it before we left, so I propped it up against the side of the trailer house.

It wasn't there!

My bicycle wasn't just important to me, it was the perfect bike. The body was a green metallic color with glitter embedded in the paint. It sparkled like diamonds when I rode around the neighborhood on sunny days. If that wasn't enough to identify it as mine, I had covered the bicycle almost entirely in bumble bee stickers.

Everyone searched the yard and the neighborhood as my parents asked if I was sure I had left it against the house.

"YES!" I knew exactly where I'd left my bike, and it was gone. Someone had stolen my perfect, beautiful bicycle, and I hadn't even said goodbye.

Dad, Diane, and I went yard to yard in our trailer park to see if it might have been one of my friends borrowing it, but my bumble bee bike was gone.

After the neighborhood search turned up nothing, Diane went inside the trailer. Dad, however, was going to drive around the neighborhood and I was allowed to go along. For the first time in my life, I sat in the passenger seat as my father drove our station wagon up one street and down another.

Peering out the open window, I searched every yard until finally a tiny light flashed in our direction. It was the glitter of my bike!

"There it is," I screamed.

Dad turned the car around and pulled up to the curb in front of the house where I'd seen my bike.

"Are you sure?" he asked. From where the car was sitting, we couldn't see anything inside the gated yard. The view I'd had from the road was now obscured by trees.

"I'm positive. That's my bike! That's my bike!" I shouted. There wasn't a doubt in my mind dad would get my bicycle back from the thieves.

"Wait here," dad commanded as he turned off the engine and stepped out of the car. He walked slowly and bobbed his head every so often as he tried to peek into the yard to see if I was correct. Once he walked past the trees, there it was, glistening in the sun plain as day—my bumble bee bike.

Dad walked back the way he had gone, but instead of getting into the car, he walked up to the gate. He reached his arm over the chain link to unlatch the bolt and walked right through. I couldn't see him at first, but then I saw him on the other side of the fence carrying my bike toward the gate. He was just a few steps from the gate when a man walked out with a seven-year-old boy by his side.

Jimmy.

As soon as I saw the kid, I knew who he was. He was the neighborhood bully who always came over to the trailer park to make fun of my friends and me, or to take our things.

"That bike wouldn't look so stupid if you hadn't put those stickers all over it," Jimmy said frequently. "Gimme that bike and I can make it look cool."

"No!" I always told him to get lost before I told my mom, and he usually did. Apparently, he had visited our house while we were gone.

"What are you doing?" the grown-up angry man yelled. "Hey, put my kid's bike down, you thief!"

"*I'm* a thief?" My father was angry, but for the first time it wasn't at one of my family members. "Your goddamned kid stole my kid's bike. Didn't you fucking notice when your kid showed up with the bike?"

"That's my kid's bike." The angry man was insistent, and it felt like the two men were going to fight.

Instead, my father told the man we were going to the police, and that's just what we did.

My father was angry as we drove to the police station, but he was on my side. When he turned to me and yelled swear words it was about what he was going to do to the people who hurt me. He was on my side!

Dad had another argument ahead of him when the sheriff asked him if we had the serial number of the bike.

"Of course not!" dad replied. "Who the hell writes down the serial number for a kid's bike? The goddamned thing is covered in bumble bee stickers. It's a girl's bike."

"I'm sorry," the sheriff replied, "but without the serial number, there's not a thing I can do about it."

Never once did the sheriff look at me or ask me questions so I could tell him I knew Jimmy did it.

My father was ranting in a raised voice as we left the sheriff's office, but it didn't matter. My arch nemesis now owned my bicycle and there was nothing I could do about it.

As much as I missed my bike and mourned its loss, all I could think about for the rest of the day was that my father took my side. When the world set out to hurt me, he stepped in and came to my defense. That had never happened before, and I wondered why it was happening now.

A week after my bike had been stolen, Grandpa Olson showed up at our house with a trailer full of wood and two brand new bicycles for Diane and me. Before the day was over, our brand-new bikes were safely parked inside a brand-new shed in our front yard. The best part was that the outside had a latch that could be padlocked.

Being seven and nine years old, it wasn't long before we had our bikes propped against the shed because we spent the day using it as a playhouse. That was where my enterprising sister had an idea for a way to make money off of our beautiful shed.

Jessy's older sister had the same omnipotent power over him that Diane had over me, so they forced us into the shed. By that time, it was August and the plains of South Dakota scorched under the hot sun. I swear that shed was about 780 degrees! It didn't matter how much we protested; they made us stay inside but we could open the door for fresh air—until a customer came along. As soon as our sisters eyed a neighborhood kid, they turned into carnival barkers.

"Hey kid, you wanna see two kids kiss?" my sister would ask any child who walked past. "Give us a quarter and you can step inside the shed to see it live."

Protesting my sister's entrepreneurial adventures was a little bit like protesting Grandma Naomi's request for a concert. I could cry all I wanted, but it would only postpone the inevitable. Eventually, Jessy wanted to play "I'll show you mine if you show me yours."

"Sure," I said, but I had seen my dad and my baby brother. I knew what boys looked like.

Once there were no customers in sight, Jessy pulled down his pants to reveal the tighty-whities his mother had picked out for him. At that exact moment, dad came out to see what we were doing in the shed and was *not* happy to find Jessy with his pants down. After a good butt chewing, Jessy was sent home, and I was sent to bed. Little did I realize at the time; my surprise defender had stepped in once again.

I have no idea how much money our sisters made off of Jessy and me, but I know neither of us ever saw a nickel.

LOSING MY MARBLES

I had just finished first grade in Watertown when Mom started packing boxes for us to move to Brookings. We were only moving fifty miles away, but this move felt different. For one thing, my best friend's family had started their bus house and driven out of our lives several months earlier. How would they ever find us?

The other difference with this move was that I had friends. Even though I'd gone through the school tour in Montana, I'd really only ever gone to school in Watertown. All my friends were there. My boyfriend—who was still six years away from driving—lived there. My zoo was there.

But none of that mattered. The station wagon was packed, and the next trailer house awaited.

We moved at the start of summer so hordes of kids were playing in the street when we pulled into our new trailer court. A group of girls was playing hopscotch at the end of the row of trailers. Boys on bikes were showing each other trick moves, and an occasional mom sat in a lawn chair watching over kids.

I hated it.

Our new trailer house was nicer than the one we'd left behind. I still shared a room with my sister, but it had purple shag carpeting! The whole back of the trailer house had the same shag carpet that was even longer than Grandma Naomi's!

Since everything we owned had to fit in the station wagon for the move, it never took long to unpack my belongings. My boredom led me outside into the neighborhood of kids.

"Do you want to play marbles?" one of them shouted.

I'd never played marbles before and had no idea what the group of kids in a circle on the cement were doing, but it didn't matter. They would teach me.

"Here, I'll give you one of my marbles."

"Me, too."

"Me, too!"

Each of the kids handed over one of his or her marbles to get me started in the game, and I could watch a few rounds before it would be my turn to shoot.

I'd seen marbles before, of course, but mostly I'd just had cat's eye marbles. The ones I held in my hand were varieties I'd never seen. There was a small steel marble that was heavier than the others, a cat's eye that was three times the size of normal marbles, and a solid blue glass marble that was the prettiest thing I'd ever seen in my life. When it came my turn to shoot, I choose my beautiful blue marble ... and missed.

I had been too busy marveling at the beauty of the perfect round glass ball to notice that people who missed lost their marble. In my first round I had lost my beautiful blue marble. I would spend the rest of that summer doing everything I could to win it back.

While I was busy playing marbles on the cement, Mom was busy working. She and dad had been hired to manage one of the bars in town where dad's band played most evenings. Every morning, Mom loaded us into the station wagon and drove uptown to clean the bar from the previous night's festivities.

The clouds of smoke haunting the ceiling weren't as thick in the mornings, which revealed underlying smells I could never quite place. There was the distinct smell of syrupy fountain drinks, alcohol, and dirty air. But below the distinguishable smells included a sour under-odor that always reminded me not to take off my shoes.

Diane and I were to pick up things from the floor that were too big for the vacuum cleaner, then wipe off the tables. The best part was we were allowed to keep all the money we found underneath the tables and chairs—until Diane found a ten-dollar bill, that is. After that, a new rule went in place—we could only keep change.

There were never feathers to collect in the bar, and Diane always beat me to the money, so I mostly plinked away on the piano that always sat on the stage. I made up stories that included rabbits running away as I played high notes on the keys, and wolves chasing them when I played the low notes. In my mind, it was a beautiful sonata which I named "The Rabbit and the Wolf."

To my parents and sister, it was annoying noise.

Cleaning the bar usually only took a few hours, and I was the first one out the door whenever Mom said, "Okay, I think that does it."

As soon as we had pulled up to the trailer court, I scanned the area for my friends. It was never long before I spotted someone I knew playing in their yard. On that day, one of my boyfriends and his cousin were at the edge of my driveway. They were waiting for me!

I had two boyfriends at that time, and both had given me a ring. Larry's ring looked like a stone from another planet. It was brown with glittery sparkles throughout the rock. It shone in the sunlight like a diamond. I loved it!

Ted had given me a ring from his mother's jewelry box. It was beautiful and clearly worth a fortune. There were two large, heart-shaped glass gemstones intertwined. One was black, and one was clear.

"It's Black Hills gold and diamond," Ted explained as he handed me the ring with pride.

I'd seen my mother's diamond ring, but I had never heard of "Black Hills gold." It certainly made sense for it to be black, and the diamond was clear just like Mom's. I loved Ted's ring too.

My father, who rarely noticed my existence unless I was in the way, saw my new ring and asked about it.

"It's Black Hills gold and diamond," I proudly answered as I held out my hand for him to admire. Even at seven-years-old, I knew it wasn't the kind of ring dad would ever be able to afford for Mom.

"That's not Black Hills gold," he said matter-of-factly.

"Yes, it is," I argued. Ted had told me it was, and he had gotten it from his mother. She would certainly know what kind of ring she had.

Dad tried to explain that the black and clear stones were just cheap pieces of glass in an adjustable ring, but I was having none of it.

"You don't know," I said under my breath as I walked away from my father, who remained unconvinced my ring was priceless.

It didn't matter what he thought. I loved my ring, and I knew it was priceless, even if he didn't.

When we pulled up to our trailer that day, though, it was Larry and Elaine waiting to ask me if I wanted to play.

I turned to Mom. My grounding was over, so I recited the rules I needed to remember. As she was contemplating her answer, a neighbor walked into our yard to see if Mom was up for a cup of coffee. The visitor made Mom's answer easy.

"Don't go out of the trailer court or on the road," Mom instructed.

We played marbles on the cement for a short while, then Larry and Elaine said they had a new game of chase they wanted to play. They jumped up from the cement at the same time and ran away from my yard. I followed them as fast as I could, but they stayed just ahead of me. When we reached the field past our trailer houses, they stopped.

"This is good," Elaine said.

I could see my house in the distance when Elaine tackled me to the ground. She grabbed both my arms and pinned them to the ground over my head.

"Take off her pants!" she screamed at Larry as he tried to hold down my legs.

Fear gripped my heart like a fist and squeezed. I knew what they were going to do as Larry climbed on my legs and faced his cousin. The look on his face showed excitement, but his cousin … his cousin was going to hurt me.

Larry unzipped my pants, and as he started to pull them down over my hips, I started kicking. I kicked as hard as I could in every direction until Larry backed away with his arms up to block my wildly flailing legs. I landed a few blows, but I have no idea where they struck his body.

Larry started to cry, and his cousin let go of my arms.

As she turned to Larry, I scrambled to my feet and ran home as fast as I could, pulling my pants back in place and zipping them as I ran. I knew it would slow me down, but I had to sneak a peek behind me. No one was following.

I made it to my house and burst through the front door of our trailer. There were leaves in my hair and grass stains on my clothes. As soon as I saw my mother's face I started to cry.

"Larry and Elaine—" I took shallow breaths through my sobs that left no room for words.

"What happened?" Mom asked as she started picking things out of my hair.

My words were broken by sobs. "They … pushed me down … and … and tried to take off my pants ... and," I blubbered, "and I kicked him as hard as I could!" That was the moment my anger defeated my terror. "Then I ran home."

"Okay, it's okay," Mom assured me. "Go get cleaned up and we'll talk about it later."

I hadn't noticed our neighbor sitting with Mom at the table until after I'd vomited the contents of my afternoon. Mom's voice had no anger. It was almost like she was telling me to go wash up for dinner when she rushed me out of the room.

We never talked about it again.

The next time I saw Larry, his cousin was nowhere to be found. He walked onto my driveway as I was playing marbles with other friends.

"Can I play?" he asked, as if nothing was different.

"No," I said as I took his ring out of my pocket. I had been carrying it around, waiting until I ran into him again.

"I hate you, and you are not my boyfriend anymore."

I threw the ring onto the cement driveway and ground my foot over the top of it. The sparkly stone flew out and chipped against the cement. The metal settings folded together and bent out of shape.

"I can fix it," Larry said as he gathered the pieces of our relationship that were forever damaged.

***

While I spent my days figuring out how to navigate life and hanging out with friends, Mom was trying to figure out how to support a family of five on virtually nothing. When she came up short, she took another job. When that still wasn't enough money, she took another job. None of the jobs were instead. They were all in addition.

I saw little of my parents' responsibilities managing the bar, but I saw enough to know most of the work fell on Mom's shoulders. Although she never complained, at some point, she must have realized that too.

Since my father had served four years in the Navy, he was eligible for the GI Bill, which would allow him to go to college for free. I remember Mom telling him about the program.

"I don't give a shit if they'll PAY me to go. I'm not going to college," was always his final answer.

Next thing I knew, Mom was getting packages in the mail that included big heavy books and an adding machine.

Day after day, Mom spent her breaks from the bar doing homework and sending the tests she took in the mail. Even if I'd been astute enough to notice the packages came in my father's name, I was never the one to get the mail.

I'm not quite sure how many hours Mom had in her day back then, but as far as I could tell, she just never slept.

Diane was almost ten, so in emergency situations when no one else was available, she was our babysitter. She held Mark on her hip in a way that almost made them look like conjoined twins as he grew bigger. It worked, though, and she was a better babysitter than most.

When Mark was two, he began speaking and one of his first words was "Gooey." He couldn't say Scooter, so when he put his arms up for me to lift him, he always called out "Gooey."

Gooey turned to Goob, and that's been my nickname ever since. I'd become accustomed to different people calling me different names, so it didn't throw me off when my immediate family called me Goob. My mom's side of the family called me Scooter, but my Grandma Naomi called me Coleen because she knew I hated it.

I was still transitioning to Goob the day I broke my shoulder.

The playground at my elementary school had limited playground equipment and it was always full. The rest of the space was filled with huge wooden spools that had once held big electrical wires. Each spool stood about four feet tall, and climbing up on one was no small feat. Once you were up though the spools were connected to make a winding bridge where we often played tag.

That day, one of my classmates trapped me on the last spool, leaving me no escape. As he reached out to tag my arm, I instinctively pulled away and fell over the edge.

As soon as I fell, kids and teachers flocked around to see if I was alright. The most worried of all was the boy who had tried to tag me. I don't remember his name, but I remember his pants always hung down too low. Though I wasn't familiar with the term "plumber's crack," I was certainly familiar with the top half of his butt.

Reassuring everyone that I was fine, I stood up. My shoulder hurt a little, but nothing horrible.

Book bags hadn't been invented yet, so it was a little difficult gathering my books at the end of the day, but it was manageable.

"I'll carry them for you," "Baggy Pants" assured me as he scooped up the books on my desk.

He didn't really leave me much of a choice, but to be honest, I was starting to feel like I needed help.

My trailer house was only a few blocks from the school, but "Baggy Pants" apologized every way possible during the walk. When we finally reached the trailer court, Mom was just stepping out the trailer house door. When she saw "Baggy Pants" she probably assumed it was another boyfriend. Then he started to explain why he had carried my books home.

"Are you alright?" Mom asked as she took hold of my elbow to test the movement in my shoulder.

That hurt!

It was always me who had emergencies when Mom was in a hurry. She was running late for one of her jobs already, and the last thing she needed to deal with was an injured kid. Still, she settled me onto the couch in front of the TV and made sure I was comfortable before she left.

"Give Aunt Julie a call at the number on the fridge if Scooter gets worse, or if you need anything," Mom instructed Diane as she walked out the door.

Mom hadn't been gone long before I fell asleep on the couch. I had outgrown naps by a couple years, but for some reason I felt exhausted. When I awoke, the light coming through the windows had turned dark, and prime-time television shows were on. Disorientation from sleep made me forget I'd hurt my arm earlier in the day ... until I tried to sit up.

Normally, my arms just moved when I thought about them doing so. That was no longer the case. Nothing worked. I remembered my bad arm, but I wasn't even trying to use that one.

I tried to swing a leg off the couch, but it wouldn't move either! Nothing below my neck moved at all when I tried to coax it into action. Diane was sitting in the rocking chair with Mark.

"Hey Diane." I couldn't wait to tell my sister about the crazy thing happening to my body. "I can't move anything."

"What do you mean?" Diane had been over any sympathy for my ailments years earlier, so her voice held more disgust than concern.

"Nothin' works." By that time, I thought it was funny and laughed as I told her what was happening. "I try to move my fingers or arms and nothin' moves."

Diane stood up and put Mark in his playpen.

"Whatever," she said as she walked toward the couch to check me out. Diane knew the perfect way to test if I was faking. She did the worst, most horribly annoying thing she could do. She tickled me.

Nothing.

It was then that Diane pulled the neck hole of my shirt to the side to look at my shoulder. I couldn't see that it was entirely black and blue, but I could see in her face it looked bad.

"I'll call Aunt Julie and see if she can come over." Diane left the living room and went into the kitchen to place the call. When she came back into the living room she asked if I wanted anything.

"Chocolate milk," I answered from my petrified position.

It wasn't long before Diane came into the living room with a glass of chocolate milk and a spoon.

"Can you sit up a little?" she asked.

I concentrated with all my might but still nothing worked. "Nope."

By the time Aunt Julie arrived at our trailer house, we had come up with a solution. I was drinking my chocolate milk from one of Mark's baby bottles as Diane sat next to me on the couch holding it up. When Julie walked in the door, she must have thought we called her for nothing. We were giggling like crazy over the fact that I was as much of a baby as Mark.

Aunt Julie took me to the emergency room, but by the time the doctor came back with X-rays, Mom was there.

"Well, it looks like you have a broken shoulder, young lady." He shoved a grey film into a clip on a big white board then turned on a bright light.

"As you can see here, the bone has completely separated and moved out of position." He looked down at me briefly, then back up at Mom. "We're going to have to set it." The rest of the conversation wasn't any scarier than if he had been telling her about what he had for lunch.

"Due to the way the bone broke, we're going to have to set it inside of the other bone. The only long-term effect is that her arm will be a quarter of an inch shorter." At that point he looked down and spoke directly to me.

"Are you ready to go put your arm back in place?" was the last thing I remember anyone saying.

By the time my arm healed, Mom was graduating with a degree in bookkeeping, and I still hadn't won back my blue marble.

MOVING NOWHERE

Mom's graduation from correspondence school was the event that changed our lives. She was offered a position in my dad's hometown and, for the first time in our lives, we were moving for her opportunity rather than his.

Mom told us the house we were moving to was a lot bigger than our trailer house, but there had never been a bigger understatement. School had just ended for Christmas break, but when it started back up again, my sister and I would be going somewhere new ... again.

Although it was only twenty minutes away, it felt like we were driving forever as we drove over snow-packed roads that led to nowhere.

"Here it is," dad said as we turned onto another road with nothing on it. Way down at the end of the road was a bunch of trees, but there wasn't a house in sight.

We bounced up and down in the back seat as dad hit invisible bumps. The center of the road had weeds so tall they were higher than the hood of the car. As we approached the grove of trees, colors that turned out to be buildings started popping through.

I stared out the window in awe at everything I saw. On my left was a long white building with hundreds and thousands of windows. As we drove past that building, a big red one behind it popped into view, then another long red one!

We had spent enough time at Grandma and Grandpa Olson's farm that we knew what outbuildings were and I instantly fell in love. In addition to the chicken coop, machine shed, and hog house, there was a pump house, the barn, a garage, and of course, the house. And it was a mansion!

The house sat on the right side of the driveway, while all the outbuildings occupied the left. There was a large porch that wrapped around the entire house. There were two sidewalks! There was a balcony on the second floor!

When dad parked the car and shut off the engine, Diane and I couldn't wait to check out the property. It felt like we had won the lottery!

Instead of my sister and I sharing a room, now we could each have two. We had a yard as big as the city park and a forest filled with trees, animals, and no fences to separate me from them. It was like I had my very own zoo right outside the door.

Dad rediscovered his love of hunting and fishing. Neither sport cut down on his drinking, but he always kept the freezer full of meat. Most days it seemed like our lives were finally becoming normal.

Then, out of nowhere, the ever-elusive common denominator would set him off. A bigger house meant I had to learn to recognize sounds of anger from a lot further away.

The sound of our car pulling up to the garage in the middle of the night always scared me awake. Immediately, I would start counting. If I counted past thirty and the engine stopped but the car door hadn't opened, I knew he was drunk. If I counted past twenty after the door was opened and the car door hadn't closed, I knew he was extremely drunk. If I counted past ninety and he hadn't closed it, I knew he was falling down drunk, and I could go back to sleep. If he hadn't reached the front door by 500, I unconsciously started holding my breath. When I couldn't hold it any longer, I took small inaudible breaths, but only when absolutely necessary. I needed to hear every little sound from downstairs.

I mentally scolded my heart for beating loud enough to interfere with my listening, but it was never loud enough to drown out the noises that mattered most, the noises that soared up the stairway and into our rooms.

As I lay in my bed with the sheet pulled up to ward off monsters, I would peek through an opening I'd left and take inventory of my room. I evaluated each item to decide how much damage I could inflict with it if I ever found the courage to do so—but that was the problem. I hadn't ever found the courage. I had inventoried those same items each time the words, "Get your ass out of bed!" broke the nighttime silence. For the hundredth time, I looked at the tennis racquet standing in the corner. Could I swing it hard enough to hurt him? Would it be enough to stop him? What if he turned his rage on me? The debate inside my head always lasted longer than the beatings. The truth of the matter was, I was too scared to step in and stop him, even if I'd had the right weapon.

I was a coward.

Lying in bed, holding my breath, I became quite good at deciphering smashing sounds. I knew the loud tinkling sounds of a glass hitting the wall. I knew the dull clank of a frying pan being thrown on the floor. I recognized the crashing sounds of a shelf being knocked off the wall or a cupboard being emptied, and I knew the muffled sound objects made when they contacted my mom.

I recognized the sounds but lay frozen in fear. I could inventory my room all night long and plan a defense that would protect everyone I loved, but in the end it wouldn't make any difference at all. I was too scared to do anything except wish and pray.

"Please God," I begged night after night, birthday after birthday, "please, please God just make him die." I never made my wishes out loud. That would have made them invalid, but I also kept them quiet because I knew they were the most horrible thoughts a person could have.

The better Mom did at work, the worse dad treated her. He started drinking more and working less, which meant he was away from the house on binges more often. It didn't matter if it was one of our birthdays or Christmas Eve, we never knew if he would be coming home or not. Personally, I liked it better when he didn't.

Mark wasn't old enough for school when we first moved to "The Farm," but Diane and I walked that half mile every day after school. It didn't matter if it was one-hundred degrees above zero or thirty degrees below zero in a white-out blizzard. Half the time we'd get to the house and dad would be sitting at the kitchen table drinking a cup of coffee and smoking a cigarette. There was no reason he couldn't come to pick us up on days that were dangerous for even livestock to be outside. But he never did.

The worst walk I remember was during a blizzard in the late seventies. No one talked about the wind chill back then, but the straight temperature was twenty-five degrees below zero. My brother was in kindergarten by that time, but he'd ridden his bus home at lunchtime. The kindergarten bus was short and easier to turn around, so his driver took him all the way to the house. Our bus driver couldn't make that turn.

Mom made sure we took boots and gloves to school, but the weather hadn't been bad when we left in the morning. By the time the bus dropped us off, it was snowing sideways so hard we couldn't see, and the drifting snow made it impossible to tell what was driveway and what was ditch. We didn't even know if we were walking the right direction, and there were no trees on either side of the driveway to guide us—or protect us from the howling wind.

The gloves I'd worn that morning were loose knit and the wind blew right through them. I tried alternating the things I was carrying from one arm to the other so I could blow on one hand at a time to warm it. The steam from my breath felt good for a second, then the moisture turned to ice. We were less than halfway down the driveway when my breaths could no longer melt the ice that had formed around the yarn of my gloves.

I couldn't see anything as I high-stepped my way through snow drifts. Besides my books, I was carrying my saxophone. It began to feel like the plastic handle was covered in razor blades as I shifted it from hand to hand.

Nothing I tried brought warmth to my hands, and the tears in my eyes from the biting wind had frozen my eyelashes together. By the time we were three-fourths of the way down the driveway, I lost feeling in both hands. It was the strangest sensation in the world, and unlike anything I'd ever felt before. The first thing to happen was my fingers lost their ability to form a fist. My saxophone case crashed into the snow. At that point, I was terrified. It no longer mattered if I dropped my books. I had already dropped my saxophone. I dropped everything I had in my arms and ran as fast as I could through the snow to the house.

My fingers no longer felt like they were a part of my body. It felt like someone had attached hot dogs to my palms that were burned as if they were being held in a fire. By the time I made it to the house even my hands were dead to the world.

There was no way for me to open the door, but I could see dad sitting in his usual spot at the kitchen table drinking a cup of coffee. The front door had a large glass window which directly faced his spot. He was less than five feet away, facing me. He didn't look up. I lifted the part of my forearm with the strength that came from my burning elbow. I flung my arm against the window of the door. My hand knocked against the glass, but I only knew it from the sound. I felt nothing from mid-forearm down. I could barely see my sister through the snow as she started up the sidewalk toward the house. That was the moment dad finally opened the door.

The words "I can't feel my hands!" came blubbering out of my mouth and somehow dad understood. He took my coat and gloves off and as the fabric pulled over my skin, I could see my skin looked white from my elbow to my fingertips.

Dad hurried me into the bathroom and turned on the water as hot as it would go. He put the stopper at the bottom of the sink and plunged my lifeless hands down into the water.

At first, I couldn't even tell that my hands were in water. I was scared the feeling would never come back and I would just have flopping hands for the rest of my life. When they started to come back to life, I greatly missed the scary numb feeling. A million needles ran through the inside of my arms, stabbing me as they spread. I screamed as the burning crept toward my fingers in a reverse path of the way the numbness had spread. The new burning was a thousand times worse than the burn I felt before everything went dead.

Dad explained it was the crystalized shards of blood starting to flow through my veins that was causing my pain.

Even after the needles reached my shoulders and dissipated into nothingness, it felt like my hands were on fire. The skin on my hands had changed from the lightest I had ever seen to the brightest red I'd ever seen.

Dad rubbed my hands with a towel to help my circulation, but the friction against my skin hurt as much as the hot water. He kept telling me I just had to tough it out.

When he finished thawing my fingers, we went back into the kitchen where my sister was just coming through the door. She was covered in snow and her face was as frozen as mine had been. Even though she was burdened with her own stack of books, I asked if she'd picked up my stuff.

"No. I had my own stuff. I didn't even know what was going on." She looked in my direction and finished her defense. "You just took off running." My sister was taking off her boots by the door and leaning against the wall. She froze in place when dad spoke.

"So, you asked your sister to carry your things?" He was speaking too slowly. Extra enunciation or pauses were never a good sign. "And she was too lazy to help you out—even after your hands were frozen?"

I didn't know what to say. She had her own books to carry, and she was cold too. It wasn't her responsibility to take care of my stuff, and it wasn't her fault I didn't pick a better pair of mittens when I left the house that morning.

On the other hand, there was a good chance she didn't help me because she hated my guts.

The real question in my mind was why did we have to walk half a mile in a raging blizzard while he sat at the kitchen table doing nothing? The days of one vehicle were behind us. Mom had our Scout SUV at work in town, but we had a truck sitting right in the driveway that worked just fine.

I didn't come to Diane's defense. Instead, I watched as dad rushed across the room to where she stood and pushed her against the wall she was leaning against because one of her feet was half out of her boot.

"Get your lazy ass back up there and get your sister's things," dad screamed in his angry voice.

I wanted more than anything in the world to be strong enough to defend my sister, but I wasn't. I just stood there frozen in fear with hot dog fingers.

Silent tears dropped straight to the floor as she bent over to pull her boots back on.

My father hurt my sister because of me. He couldn't stand me, but he hurt her anyway. He was the one at fault, and he hurt her anyway! And she hated me even more because of it. I certainly couldn't blame her, and it made me wish even harder that dad would just fall off the face of the earth.

From that day on, if the weather was bad, we went to Mom's office and waited to go home with her at the end of the workday. The farm implement company where she worked was also a car dealership, and the place was huge! We could sit on carpeted benches and do our homework. Sometimes Mom would even pay me to help her do filing. Since we lived in an agriculture-based community, Kneip Implement was a gathering place for anyone and everyone in the area.

One of my favorite things to do was to just sit and watch people. The most fascinating people to me were the members of the family who owned it. In my eyes, they were the epitome of upper class in our new hometown in the middle of nowhere.

A MILLION TINKLES

The Kneip family was the closest thing our little town had to royalty. Not only was one of the brothers the owner of the business where several family members worked, another brother was governor of the state. To me, they were the Kennedys of South Dakota and everything about them fascinated me.

It didn't matter if it were a grandchild to the original owner or the governor himself, every family member had a confidence I envied to my core. They all had a natural ability to make whomever they were talking to feel like the most important person in the world. That was probably why I enjoyed being around them so much.

It wasn't that they spent the time I was there making me feel better about myself. For the most part, I just blended into whatever furniture I was sitting in after they had said an initial hello. I loved to study them. I loved listening to how they said what they said, then in turn, how people reacted to what was said. The main car salesman was the owner's brother, and he truly could sell ice to an Eskimo.

"Shoot ... with all your money, what are you doing driving an old car like that?" the salesman asked.

The farmer looked down at the ground and kicked a little at the gravel. I noticed his face had turned red.

"You know what a guy like you needs?" By this time, the salesman had his hand on the farmer's shoulder and was leading him to a new car on the lot. "A guy like you belongs in a Cadillac."

"I don't know ..." The farmer pulled off his feed cap and scratched the messy hair on top of his head. "That's a lot of money for a car."

"Oh sure," the salesman replied, "not everybody can be a Caddie person. I just thought you were one. I tell you what. Let's just take it for a drive. You gotta at least drive once in your life."

I knew as soon as the two men crawled into the Cadillac that the farmer would be buying it before Mom finished work, and I was right.

Unfortunately, "Cadillac People" are like "White Pants People." Not everyone can be one, and this gentleman had his Caddie repossessed a couple of months later when he couldn't make the payments.

The Kneips weren't like other salespeople I'd seen in my life who flatter you like crazy to your face, and then bash you to everyone else the second you leave. They spoke just as kindly about the people who weren't there as the ones who were. I wanted to be like them more than anything in the world. I also knew I never could be.

My world was a continuous parade of supporting characters who moved in and out like storms. The Kneips had dignity and roots that were respected in our little town. My roots were, at best, prune-able.

I started looking forward to crappy weather so I could stay in town and hang out at the implement dealer, but most days we still had to take the bus home after school.

One day when the bus dropped us off, we were met by an old pickup truck coming up the driveway from our house. We walked up to the driver's door as he cranked down the window.

"Yer dad home?" the elderly man who looked like Santa Clause in bib overalls asked.

I remember thinking what an incredibly stupid question to ask when we obviously just came home. And why wouldn't he know? Didn't he just come from there?

I knew better than to be as rude as my thoughts wanted me to be, so I held my tongue.

"We don't know," Diane answered. "We just got home from school, but we can go see."

"Santa" offered us a ride down the driveway, and we gladly accepted. Diane opened the passenger door and I crawled into the middle. A large German shepherd was pacing in the bed of the pickup but stopped as soon as "Santa" started the truck moving again.

As soon as we pulled into the yard, we could see dad's truck was gone. "Santa Claus" said he wanted to wait and asked if that would be alright.

We were used to strangers dropping by our house to see dad. Sometimes they were musicians and sometimes they were acquaintances looking for permission to hunt on our land. Nothing about our bearded visitor seemed out of the ordinary.

I noticed the man had a shotgun propped next to his leg when I crawled in the truck, but it was more out of a reminder to myself to be careful than any real concern. My father drove around with a loaded gun next to his leg all the time. It was always hunting season in our shelterbelt and the gravel roads around us.

Diane, Mark, and I sat with him at the kitchen table while we did our homework. He fiddled with a guitar he'd brought along and sang a few songs we knew. His German shepherd was either old or exhausted, because he just slept at "Santa's" feet the entire time. He didn't even stir when our little house dog sniffed around him to see if he wanted to play.

"Santa" started all his songs with "Hey, have you heard this one?" and usually ended with "Did your dad ever tell you about …?" Homework became a low priority as he told us stories about his life. I forgot about school entirely when he started talking about what he'd been doing the past few days.

Computers were still something that were only used by huge companies or the government, but "Santa" told us he knew how to work them. He tapped his temple as he winked.

"They locked me up over there at Yankton, in the nut house." He chain-smoked as he told his tale. "The nurses hand out medicine at the same time every night, so after they left my room, I went over to their computer and erased myself." "Santa" explained how he'd hacked into the institute's computer system and removed his name from the patient list. After that, he simply walked out the door and there was nothing they could do about it.

He wasn't "Santa." He was James Bond!

I imagined him using super spy devices to crack open safes. I pictured him dressed in a dark suit and holding a briefcase as he strolled out of the asylum. He laughed at how simple it was to pull the wool over everyone's eyes and I marveled at his story. He tried to explain the process a little bit, but I'd never even seen a computer. All I really learned was that he was a genius!

Mom came home after work the same time she usually did and spent the rest of the evening hearing the stories we'd already heard "Santa" tell. She invited him to join us for dinner, at which he regaled us with even more stories of his life.

Eventually it was time for my siblings and me to go to bed. For the most part, the evening wasn't that much different than a dozen other nights we had spent with people who were waiting for dad to come home.

When I awoke in the morning, our bearded friend was gone. As always, a great deal of Mom's life happened after I went to bed.

After "Santa" and his dog settled into the bed in our den and fell asleep, Mom started calling bars to find my father. She finally tracked him down after one in the morning and described our visitor.

Dad told her to call the police.

Mom asked the police not to turn on lights or sirens because there were children sleeping. We heard nothing when the sheriff and his deputy found "Santa" sleeping with his dog on one side and his shotgun on the other.

I never found out why "Santa" tracked dad down to our remote house in the country, or why he wouldn't let Mom put his shotgun somewhere safe when he went to sleep. All I knew was that another eccentric friend of dad's had come and gone.

Dad was always kinder when he had friends in the house. When it was just us, Mom received the worst of dad's temper. Don't get me wrong, there was always plenty left over for the rest of us.

One of his favorite pastimes was thinking of new ways to insult us.

My favorite of his sayings was always, "If you don't knock it off, I'm going to hit you so hard your relatives will feel it!" It was my favorite because I believed it to be a perfect example of his stupidity. He apparently didn't understand the logic loop in his joke: he would be hurting himself. Duh.

When I had first started school, dad's favorite nickname for me was "Dumb Shit." I must have been a faster learner than he expected though, because by the time I was in sixth grade I had been promoted to "Smart Ass." For the most part, I just tried to stay out of his way.

One day after school he ordered my sister and me to do the dishes because Mom "shouldn't have to do everything around this house." It must not have occurred to him to do them himself while he was home alone all day, but I knew bringing that up would just make things worse. I wasn't about to start anything with him.

My sister was washing, I was drying, and we were arguing as usual. She didn't think I was rinsing them correctly, and I thought she should either leave me alone or do them herself. We were both more wrapped up in our argument than our job. We were also too busy to notice dad watching.

He came up from behind, pushed us to each side, scooped the unwashed dishes out of the sink and threw them all on the floor. Shards of glass and puddles of soapy water ran down into the furnace vent below the sink and pooled in low spots of the linoleum.

Both Diane and I tried to clean up the mess, but he wouldn't let us.

"I want your mother to see how worthless you both are when she gets home," dad screamed. "She works all day, then she has to come and take care of your lazy asses."

Of course, even after he'd made sure Mom saw his evidence of our worthlessness, it wasn't like he cleaned the mess. He didn't even make us do it!

Mom cleaned the mess, then made dinner, then cleaned the kitchen after dinner. The whole time Mom slaved away in the kitchen she was forced to listen to his tirade about how lazy and good for nothing her children were.

I woke in the middle of the night to glass exploding against the kitchen walls. The tinkling and clanking were loud, and probably dangerous, but from my vantage point not that scary. He wasn't drunk, and he wasn't hurting Mom. He was just emphasizing each of his talking points about our laziness by breaking something.

He wasn't mad at her. He was mad at us. That was good! Eventually his tantrum ended, and the house fell asleep.

I walked downstairs the next morning for breakfast as if it were any other day, but Mom stopped me at the kitchen door. She was holding my shoes and told me I needed to put them on before I went into the kitchen.

As I peered into the kitchen it looked like a diamond mine. Every surface of the room, from the highest shelf to the floor itself, glittered with thousands of glass shards.

"Kinda pretty, isn't it?" Mom said lightly. She told me she was going to leave them to see how long it would take dad to clean them up. It was the first time I'd ever heard Mom give any indication she disapproved of dad's antics. Of course, dad would die before losing a battle of wills, so the glass hadn't been on the floor more than a day before Mom started the cleanup that would never really end. Decades later, we still found tiny pieces of glass in the nooks and crannies of the kitchen.

The night of a million tinkles was the night we switched to wooden bowls, paper plates, and plastic glasses.

WEAKENING MAGNETIC FORCE

Looking back, dad may just have been striving for shock appeal, because his need to make us miserable surfaced in the oddest ways. One of them was his cooking phase. He had bought a 150-year-old cookbook at an auction and decided it would be fun to try some of the recipes. It had been written in the days when nothing was wasted, so we ate everything from raccoon stew to chicken feet.

Eating something other than what was prepared for us—or even going without dinner—were not options so my sister, brother, and I became skilled at discreetly disposing of food. It was particularly challenging because much of what dad made was so disgusting our dogs wouldn't take it when we tried to sneak it to them under the table.

My brother's trick was to ask to go to the bathroom. Parents can never say no to a bathroom request. He would take a huge mouthful of food before standing up, then spit it out in the toilet.

Unfortunately, my gag reflex was far too keen to keep my arch nemesis of foods—squash—in my mouth long enough to get to the bathroom. My trick was to slide the source of my disgust between the layers of paper plates. We bought the cheap ones with about 30,000 plates in a package, so it always took four or five to hold the food. I became a master at squishing squash between the layers.

My sister's solution was to douse everything with enough ketchup to make it edible.

On the surface, cooking seemed like a helpful hobby for dad to take on. At least it was taking one of the countless chores off Mom's shoulders. Well, that might have been true if it hadn't been for the mounds of pans, utensils, splatters, and spills that the culinary master left for his exhausted wife to clean.

Then one day when we came home from school, the most amazing aroma met us at the door. Dad was cooking roast beef, mashed potatoes, and corn. Finally! After weeks of experimentation, he made an edible meal! I was so happy I had to fight back tears.

My siblings and I went to our rooms to do homework and wait to be called down to dinner. The whole time I was doing homework, the mouthwatering scent of my absolute favorite meal wafted through the floor vents directly into my room. Ours was a 125-year-old house, and the only heat upstairs came from holes in the floor, covered with wrought iron grates.

When it was finally time to eat, I was starving. All three of us ran down the stairs like a herd of elephants. We rounded the corner into the kitchen and saw bowls of what looked like diarrhea at each of our places on the table.

My heart sank into my stomach as I looked at the bowl of something that would be way harder to swallow than squash. I'd been so excited, then so very disappointed that I couldn't stop myself from voicing my complaints.

"What?" I stood frozen, staring at the bowls of brown puree. "What happened to the roast and potatoes?" I asked.

"Just sit down," dad commanded. "I put the roast, potatoes, and corn in the blender." He dipped his spoon into the thick sludge and took a bite.

My mind screamed NO! And I couldn't stop my eyes from filling with tears.

Why couldn't he have just done that with his own meal and left ours alone? Why did he have to ruin everything?

He must have achieved the shock he was hoping for because his spirits were high as he watched me stare at my bowl. Regardless of the way I looked at my bowl, there was no possible way I would be able to eat my "soup" without throwing up on the table.

Dad laughed at the comparison to diarrhea I was making. Of course, that still didn't mean eating it was optional; it just meant I could complain without setting him off, so I did.

Dad joked, "It all winds up in the same place anyway."

No matter how many times I brought a spoonful of the gook up to my mouth, I gagged. The more I stared at my bowl, the more nauseous I became. The table was silent as everyone else, including dad, tried their bowl of dinner.

"Just put ketchup on it," Diane said as she ate a spoonful of what now looked like bloody diarrhea in her bowl. My sister always knew what was best for me, regardless of what I wanted. Before I could stop her, she covered my bowl in a thick layer of ketchup.

That did NOT make it look more appetizing, but it did give me a brilliant idea. Since I wasn't the one who put the ketchup in my bowl, he had to let me out of eating it. I pitched my new argument that Diane had ruined my dinner. As far as I was concerned, I had an airtight case.

Much to my delight, it worked!

"Fine, then don't eat it," dad said. The humor he'd shown about the situation a few minutes earlier was gone. "But you can sit there until everyone else is done eating."

That was fine by me.

Dad stood up and walked in between where my sister and I were sitting to take my bowl. He picked it up, and I assumed he was going to put it on the counter.

I should have taken my own bowl to the counter.

Dad cupped my bowl in his hand as he removed it from the table, but instead of taking it away he slammed it upside down on my sister's head. He then ground the bowl fiercely, as if he were screwing it on the top of her skull.

I sat next to my sister for the rest of the dinner.

No one spoke as the brown and red mixture dripped down her face and clothes. No one spoke as the tears coursed silently down her cheeks. No one spoke at all. But I didn't need words to know that it was my fault my sister had been hurt ... again.

Dad was a master at personalizing punishments for each of us. Mine were always that someone else would have to pay for my mistakes. Maybe it was because I was too fragile, and he knew physical punishments might break something. Maybe it was because he knew I would tell the truth when the doctor asked who hurt me. Maybe he just learned early that manipulative mind games worked better on me.

His manipulation wasn't limited to punishments though.

I was around ten when dad came home with a tiny piglet from the sale barn. The baby was free because it had a ruptured stomach and would likely die in a few days.

"If anybody can nurse this little guy back to health, you can," dad said.

I was speechless. He was telling me I was good at something. He was saying, indirectly, he believed in me. He'd never trusted me with anything before, and I would do anything necessary to take care of my baby pig which, of course, I named Porky.

My days began an hour earlier than normal so I could feed Porky before school.

Maybe he heard the bus drop us off a half mile away, but Porky aways knew when I reached the bottom of our driveway. He frantically snorted and squealed until I ran to the pig house for his afternoon feeding.

I started by feeding him milk from a bottle, but he grew fast. Before long, he was huge and snorting up more than two gallons of milk a day. He ate other food by then, of course, but milk was his favorite. We couldn't afford to give him real milk, so I mixed water and powdered milk. He loved it just as much.

I spent so much time with Porky that my dog started snorting to get back some of the attention she'd lost.

One day after school, I was surprised at what I didn't hear. Porky wasn't squealing as I came down the driveway. I thought about just running down to check on him, but I knew better than to go see him without some milk.

I mixed his jug of instant milk as dad sat at the table reading the paper. After I had everything ready, I headed off to the pig house. As I walked down the hill, Porky still wasn't making any noise. My stomach filled with knots and began to hurt. I knew something was wrong before I even reached the door.

Porky was gone! I searched the inside of the building, calling his name. There wasn't a sound in response. I searched the outside of the building. I searched the entire yard yelling his name, but he was nowhere to be found. Porky was gone. Had I forgotten to close a door?

I walked into the house, expecting the worst when I told dad that Porky was gone. He looked up at me from the paper he was reading with a smirk, and I understood.

He already knew.

"He's as big as he's gonna get and there's no sense payin' to feed him," dad said flatly. "I took him down to the butcher this afternoon."

The butterflies in my stomach turned acidic and I wanted to throw up. Porky was gone, and I didn't even get a chance to say goodbye. I had an entire gallon of milk mixed and no one to give it to. I looked down at the jug as my first tear splashed against its side.

I set the jug on the counter next to the sink and went up to my room. I couldn't look my father in the eye and there was nothing left to say.

He had all the power and I had none.

To add insult to injury, he had taken pork chops out of the freezer for Mom to make for dinner. For years, I believed it was Porky being served for dinner that night as I tried to choke down what I was served. It wasn't until adulthood I realized the processing of an animal doesn't happen that quickly.

***

Mind bruises were easier to hide than physical bruises, but they didn't hurt any less. Every time I let myself believe my father was being kind, he was simply setting me up for a fall.

As I hid my mental bruises, Mom tried to hide the black and blue marks dad frequently left on her face. She was in a professional position at a company where nearly everyone in town stopped by at least once a week. Her secret was becoming harder to hide.

Her boss valued her enough to help with anything she needed, regardless of what it was, but that seemed to fuel dad's anger. For the first time in his life, dad realized how much better Mom's life would be without him. While it would still take over a decade for my father's pull on my mother to break, his magnetism was beginning to weaken.

As for me, I was aluminum.

SOMETHING OLD AND SOMETHING NEW

Around the time I entered middle school, my Grandpa Olson had a heart attack. Fearing the worst, the adults all rushed to the hospital. Even my father went, and he never went to anything on the Olson side.

My sister, brother, and I sat at home waiting for answers no one had thought to give us. Diane had been taking care of us long enough to know how to feed us and get us into bed, but none of us knew how to go to sleep with unanswered questions. It was way past dark when the car pulled up in the driveway.

As always, I held my breath and listened for every sound. The first car door opened, and I automatically started counting in my head. A second car door opened, then a third and I wondered who could be visiting this time of night?

All three of us ran downstairs to find out what was going on with Grandpa, but also who the third person was going to be. We made it to the kitchen just as they were coming in the front door. Dad was first, followed by our Aunt Lillian, and Mom bringing up the rear.

It was late, and no one felt like re-living the day they had just gone through, but my siblings and I were dying to know.

"How's Grandpa?" "What's going on?" "Where's Grandma?" "Is Lily staying now?" "Where is she going to sleep?" "What's going on with Grandpa?" Diane, Mark and I fired questions at Mom without giving her a moment to answer.

Finally, Mom gave in and told us he had gone through surgery to replace one of his heart valves with a pig's heart valve.

Dad immediately cracked a joke about whether Grandpa would start "oinking," which made Lily laugh. Everything he said made Lily laugh. She loved my father.

Mom joked along as Diane joined in, and I knew Grandpa was going to be alright. No one would be laughing if he were going to die. I did, however, wonder how long Lily would be with us. More importantly, I needed to know where she was sleeping. I did not want to be tickled awake at two in the morning ever again! Fortunately, Mom made up a bedroom in the den. It turned out Grandpa would have to stay in the hospital for several weeks.

In his retirement, he had started an antique business that operated from their farm. Every outbuilding was filled with priceless treasures, like a Timex case with shelves inside that turned around to show tiny treasures. There were old pointy shoes, and a horse-drawn carriage—or, in our case, a sibling-drawn carriage. Everywhere you looked in the granary, the pig house, the barn, and even the shelterbelt were antiques that people came from far and wide to purchase.

Grandpa never had a retail store, but he gained customers from word of mouth and the occasional flea market. He only did the "big" flea markets that were held outdoors in the summer. Grandpa would load a trailer with tables and boxes filled with some of the treasures from his farm.

One of the biggest "shows" was happening while Grandpa was still in the hospital recovering. The big outdoor shows were incredibly difficult to get into as a vendor, and if Grandpa didn't show up, someone else would take his spot the following year. Not wanting that to happen, he asked Mom to cover his booth.

That must have been all it took for Mom to get the flea market bug, because we continued to do at least five flea markets each year long after Grandpa recovered and could have taken over. Mom still worked at the implement dealership during the week, but her "free time" now included researching items dad found at garage sales, auctions, abandoned houses, or our favorite shopping location—the dump.

Being a vendor at a flea market gave us access to everything the venue had to offer—even the areas that weren't open to the public.

Diane only lived at home for a couple of years during the flea market era, but Mark and I spent three weekends each summer sleeping in a tent and helping our parents run their antiques booth. For the most part, they just wanted us to stay out of the way.

Mark and I had free rein at whatever site was hosting the show. We just had to check in every so often to make sure our parents didn't need help or a potty break. While our parents were busy selling antiques, my friends and I were busy doing whatever seemed interesting.

One of the outdoor shows was held at a place made up to resemble an antique town. There were buildings filled with costumed mannequins where visitors could see what life had been like in the previous century. There was a carousel where my sister and I both worked to make money. Most importantly, this place had an antique passenger train. One of our favorite things to do was secretly lock ourselves in one of the first-class cabin cars and laugh as tourists tried to open the door. When they couldn't get it open, they always theorized what could possibly be inside that was so important they'd need to lock it up. We'd hang out in those cars for hours, laughing and smoking cigarettes.

Life at the flea markets was different than life at home in almost every way. I had a flea market friend who ran the streets in an actual city. I had another friend who smoked pot in his van after he was finished helping his parents with evening attended by the rest of our parents. These were the friends who wouldn't judge my struggles or my experimentation.

Back home, my friends were the good kids.

My very best friends in the world were Julie and Traci. We did everything together. We were in the same clubs, on the same teams, in the same classes, and at night we spent hours on the phone. I slept countless nights at either Julie's or Traci's house, and our favorite pastime was roller-skating.

Every weekend, we begged our parents to drive us the twenty miles to the rink. Whistling Wheels was the hottest place to be on a Saturday night, and among the three of us, we usually found a driver.

It wasn't just the skating that caught our attention, of course, it was also the two brothers who worked the rink most weekends. Tim and Pete were not only the best skaters we had ever seen in our lives, but they were also gorgeous. Considering how low my heart sank if we arrived at the rink and Tim wasn't working, skating was not my main priority. On the days we paid our admission and rounded the corner to see him behind the counter, my heart soared.

He had dark brown feathered hair and blue eyes that seemed to shine with his interest in me. I wanted so badly to believe that mine were the only eyes he looked at that way, but reality always became apparent at the couple's skate. Halfway through the evening, the DJ would clear the floor and the lights would dim. A disco ball at the center of the ceiling spun dazzling flashes around the rink as all the girls waited to be chosen.

Well, not all the girls. Some nights a girl would race up to Tim and ask him for the couple's skate before he had a chance to leave his work area. He was always too nice to say no.

Then there were the heartbreaking nights when he asked someone else.

Julie and Traci knew how I felt, of course. I talked about Tim nonstop. How did he feel? Why did he ask me to skate most of the time, but not others? Does he like me? Why doesn't he ever ask me out?

The only times those questions weren't rattling around my brain were the times he was in my arms. Since he could do any kind of trick skating, it was easy for him to go backwards. My hands around his neck felt the softness of his hair. Our bodies would be close enough that it was more like dancing—until one of my inevitable screw ups. Any time we fell, Tim instinctively landed in a way that sacrificed himself and protected me. Surely that was love, wasn't it?

Regardless, our relationship rarely appeared in my life off the skates. Tim never asked me out on a date, but he and a friend came to my house to hang out one day. He didn't need directions. He didn't need directions! How could he not need directions and still never ask me out on a date?

Over the years, I learned that Tim only asked me to skate when he was between girlfriends. He'd never even asked me out on a date, for crying out loud! Once again, my shortcomings were things other people could see but I couldn't. Was it just … everything about me? My house was filled with ghosts of people who'd owned the thousand antiques before we did, and my heart was filled with the ghost of Tim.

Would there ever be a time in my life when I'd find something new?

NOW YOU'RE GONNA GET IT

I remember the last time my father beat my mother.

I was fifteen. I still don't know what set him off, but it probably had to do with his jealousy over someone who encountered Mom. This particular rampage was a bad one.

As I lay in my bed holding my breath so I could hear better, I tried to muster the courage to get up and stop him. Eventually Mom's screams and pleas for him to stop turned to silence. I tried to listen further and deeper, then I heard the first step of the staircase creak.

The movement was slow and torturous. I imagined dad coming up the stairs with a butcher knife to finish off the rest of us. There were fourteen steps in that old stairwell, and I counted each one as I searched my room for a hiding place that didn't exist. I pulled the sheet completely over my head.

I peeked between my blankets and saw the final step. It was Mom!

She was wearing a white vinyl trench coat tied at the waist. The bottom half of her nightgown poked out from under her coat, and I could see she was wearing boots. Mom was holding a bloody paper towel to her face and had tissues stuck up both of her nostrils. Several other places were still bleeding, but it was coming from too many injuries for her to catch it all. Blood dripped and splattered down the front of her white plastic coat.

Diane, Mark, and I ran to her in relief.

"Get some clothes on," Mom said in a nasal voice because of the tissues. "We're leaving."

Halleluiah!

Suddenly, everything else seemed fixable. We were all together and we were getting out! We grabbed the things we needed for the night and gathered at the top of the stairs. Mom's strength had given me the nudge I needed to grab my tennis racquet from the corner. If anyone tried to stop us, I would be ready to protect us all and bash the offender right in the head.

I was first in line as we started down the enclosed staircase. It was a typical old farmhouse, so the stairway was literally a hole in the floor walled in on all sides. It was open at the top and bottom. I could only see a short distance past the doorway until I was halfway down. Even then, I couldn't see anything but the carpet on the main floor. I had no idea what might be right next to the wall on either side at the bottom.

When I reached the fourth step from the bottom, my father pivoted from out of sight to the center of the doorway. His arms were crossed, and he was blocking our only way out.

Dad looked me in the eyes and said calmly, "Go back upstairs. You aren't going anywhere."

But Mom said we were, and I had the tennis racquet. I didn't even blink when I looked at him with all the hatred I had and said, "Get the hell out of the way."

Much to my surprise—he did!

I'm sure I stood dumbfounded for at least a second before I gathered my courage and started down the remaining stairs. I expected him to reach out and grab me as I turned toward the kitchen, but he didn't.

Of course… it wasn't me he wanted to stop.

When Mom walked out of the stairway, he grabbed her arm. Even with my tennis racquet, I'd failed her. We watched as dad tried to apologize and ask Mom if they could just go into the other room and talk for a while. He wiped blood from her face like he would take care of her. She jerked her arm back and walked away.

Dad followed her through the kitchen, but when she went out the front door, it was sprinkling. He didn't have any shoes on, so he stopped. He likely figured it didn't matter. She would come back.

My siblings and I watched from the living room wondering if we should go or stay. We were still talking about our options when we heard the car start outside. We saw the headlights in the window as it drove away and turned back to look at each other. Mom had left, and we were alone... with the monster.

"Mom's not coming back, you know," Diane said. "We gotta call Grandma."

We agreed the only solution was for me to call Grandma Naomi. They lived the closest and the monster was her son. I would make the call, even though she hated me most of all.

I thought back to the Pepto-Bismol and the dark hallway to the bathroom in our old trailer. I wanted to tell Grandma about her precious son's behavior even less than I'd wanted to walk that dark hallway. But my sister was right. Someone had to do it.

We walked as quietly as we could into the den at the back of our house. It wasn't heated but it had a telephone, and we could call for help. I dialed the numbers, and after several rings, Grandma answered the phone.

"Could you come out to the house?" I asked quietly.

"Why?" she asked in her sharp manner. "Is everyone alright?"

"We just ..." I couldn't possibly say it over the phone. "Could you please come out?" I asked again.

She wasn't happy about it, but she agreed to come out to our house.

Diane, Mark, and I huddled in the den for a long time but heard no sounds from the rest of the house. Eventually we made our way back to the living room. The window reflected dad sitting in the kitchen with his elbows on the table, his head in his hands. He was in the sorry stage. We would be safe until our grandparents arrived.

One of us kept an eye on the darkness outside for the headlights that would signal our escape with Grandma and Grandpa. Revealing the family secret we'd held for so long was probably punishable by death.

On the other hand, it might also mean salvation.

Dad would know I was the one who called them, but it wouldn't matter. They could protect us. Everything would be fine because someone would finally know what was going on.

We saw the small dots of light turn into the driveway, but only because we were watching out the window. Dad didn't see their car until it pulled up to our garage. Even then, he assumed it was Mom.

It was amazing how easily he could turn off the devastating remorse he'd been feeling at the table and turn on the charismatic charm when he greeted his parents at the door.

"What are you guys doing here?" he asked his parents. Rather than answer his question, they both looked toward the three of us standing in the kitchen doorway. Dad turned to follow their gaze and looked me straight in the eye. He knew.

Grandma made us all sit down at the kitchen table together. My eyes squinted in hatred as I looked at my father. I hated that he could pretend he didn't know why we would have called them.

Now you're gonna get it." I thought to myself.

The only person scarier than dad was Grandma. He tried to act as if their sudden visit meant nothing, but he gave his nervousness away when he started turning everything he said into a joke or one-liner. Just as we all took our seats around the table, a second car pulled up to the garage.

Mom was back.

The room went silent when Mom walked in the door. The sprinkles of rain hadn't washed the blood away. It was spread down the front of her coat. She looked like she'd been in a car accident. Her white vinyl coat was dripping pink liquid along the bottom hem where her blood had mixed with the rainwater. Dark red streams of blood were continually fed by drips from her nose and lip. One of her eyes was nearly swollen shut, and her hair was caked with dried blood.

Dad was finally going to be in big trouble. I waited for Grandma's reaction ... a reaction that never came.

I at least expected one of them to jump up and help Mom in some way. I stared open-mouthed from adult to adult around the table. I expected someone to ask what happened. I expected someone to gasp. I expected someone to jump up and grab my father by the collar. Neither of them did any of those things.

Had I fallen into some alternate universe?

Mom was carrying a bucket of take-out chicken and placed it on the table as Grandma, Grandpa, and dad made stupid small talk about how good the chicken smelled. Nobody freaked out and screamed, "What the hell is going on?" They barely even noticed Mom was bleeding!

I finally understood.

They knew. They had always known.

Grandma and Grandpa weren't surprised by Mom's appearance because they'd always known what was going on in our house. They knew what their son was doing to all of us, and they did nothing.

Grandma asked Mom to sit with us at the table. I watched and listened with disbelief and growing fury as my grandmother spoke. She explained how our actions were provoking uncharacteristically violent behavior in dad. She explained what a "better" family would do in our situation. She spent a great deal of time and gave us a substantial number of examples to prove that what happened was our fault. She was telling us exactly what my father had always said. She used the exact words that had run through my mind all my life to describe our worthlessness.

Hearing those words out loud—and directed at someone other than just me—I realized how utterly stupid they were.

"How can you look at Mom and say that?" I pointed my arm toward my mother, then glared at my grandmother. "How can you take his side?"

My 300-pound grandfather sat mute, staring at my 90-pound grandmother.

I was appalled. The Cavalry had arrived—and they trampled us.

I had lain in bed for fifteen years wishing I had the courage to step in, wishing I had the courage to tell someone what dad was doing to Mom. When it was finally out, I watched as my scary grandmother and 300-pound grandfather took his side.

"He couldn't help it," Grandma explained.

I had seen my father attack my mother for absolutely no reason, with absolutely no provocation. I had seen my father drag my mother out of bed by her hair to make him a sandwich after he came home drunk at 2:00 am.

My grandparents were wrong. I didn't just think they were wrong; I KNEW they were. I shook my head and started to argue again when my grandmother interrupted, "Your father loves you to death."

I'd had enough.

I said, definitively, "Well, we hate his guts." I rose from the table and started toward the door when my grandfather finally spoke.

"Don't talk back to your grandmother."

I turned to look in his direction. "Pffft, go to hell." I waved a hand dismissively in my grandparents' general direction. I don't know if that was significant in their minds, but it was in mine. It was a wave of erasure over people who were no longer my family.

My grand departure had the profound impact of absolutely nothing. They finished whatever conversation came next while I sat in my room, taking my stand alone. I was silently protesting a wrong that no one else seemed to even find significant.

There were countless ways I could have responded to the failed intervention. I could have been sympathetic to my grandparents, who had to face the reality they didn't raise a perfect child. I could have felt badly for my dad, who was obviously embarrassed in front of his parents. Instead, I decided to hate them all. They knew the unequivocal fact that my dad had hurt my mom, and they did nothing. That night as I said my prayers for my father to die, I added a request that my father and his parents someday get what they deserved.

AIN'T GOT TIME

Just like the hundreds of other times my father had senselessly beaten my mother, the events of that evening were never discussed again.

Dad started doing more projects around the house and in the garage. He was in the remorse stage and did everything he could to suck up to Mom. Projects he'd been promising to do for years were suddenly active again. Whether it was repairing the wobbly leg on the kitchen table or building an icehouse behind the garage, dad was doing everything he could to demonstrate his worth.

I would learn later that my parents had gone to our minister for counseling during this time. Mom never shared the topics they discussed, but she did say that in the minister's decades-long service at the church, she and dad were the only couple to whom he recommended divorce. Of course, dad was going to prove him wrong with his best behavior.

***

One summer day while dad was working in the garage, I decided to put some fresh flowers inside the house. I was outside picking wildflowers when our neighbor drove up on his tractor with his five-year-old son. Dad came out of the garage to greet them.

"You gonna take me fishin' today?" Adam had been asking dad to take him fishing since the beginning of summer, but dad always had some excuse why he couldn't.

"Oh, I can't today. I'm too busy. Maybe next week though," dad answered.

Dad and the neighbor visited for a bit, but I went back to picking wildflowers. The irises, lilies, and lilacs were in endless bloom around our ten-acre yard. I never really cared whether something was a tall weed or an actual flower if the blossoms were pretty.

By the time I had a huge armload of flowers I lost track of what my father and the neighbors were doing. I walked into the kitchen and spread my collection across the kitchen table. Just as I started searching cupboards for vases, the phone rang.

"Hello," I answered.

"Put your dad on the phone. Adam's dead." It was Grandma Naomi.

"What?" I replied. I had just seen Adam a few minutes ago. There was no way he could be dead. I didn't think he'd even left the yard yet. My mind was spinning with questions, but Grandma had no time for me.

"Put…your…father…on…the…phone…Adam is dead!" She enunciated each word and they landed like punches to my heart. She had to be wrong!

I set the phone down and walked out of the house in a trance. Halfway between the house and our garage, I heard the ambulance. I saw the lights as it drove by the end of our driveway. I stared in disbelief until it was out of sight, then I turned back to the garage to tell dad to pick up the phone.

Dad went over to the neighbor's house to see if he could help with anything, but he wouldn't let me go. I went back to the kitchen and arranged my flowers … in shock.

I had babysat Adam since he was a tiny baby. I was the one watching him when, at three years old, he came to me with a tall tumbler of Kool Aid and said, "I've got some Koooooool Aid."

The way he said it made me suspicious, so I asked to smell it. As I suspected, it was a full glass of wine that he'd poured for himself from behind his parents' bar! The worst part was that I didn't want them to think I drank it, so I had to pour it back into the bottle.

He was five years old. Five-year-olds don't die!

He was the kid who gave me the scare of my life when, at four years old, he said there was a man in his closet. Our houses were five miles from town, and I was only thirteen.

Adam shook in terror as he cried about the person waiting in his room. He described who he'd seen and hugged my legs.

I had no idea what to do, so I called my house. There was no answer. I called my sister, who was married and living on her own by then, but she didn't answer her phone either! I scanned the living room for items I could use as a weapon while I thought about who else I could call.

It was then I heard Adam and his sister on the stairway.

"Do it one more time and I think she'll let us sleep downstairs." His older sister was the director and Adam was the Academy Award-deserving performer of the year.

That boy could not be dead. I wasn't even sure I was done being mad at him about the boogeyman story. There was no way he could be gone.

Grandma was always the first to know about tragedies because my grandfather was on the volunteer fire department. He had a scanner that broadcast the news about Adam as it called for first responders. Adam had been run over by the milk truck and hadn't survived.

Grandma was never happier than when she was the first to know and spread horrible news. She was abrupt with me because she needed to relay the information quickly. After all, she had more people to notify.

Adam's death affected all of us, but as with every tragedy we never talked about it. The only time I heard dad talk about his feelings was once when his friends were sitting at the kitchen table drinking beer. I accidentally eavesdropped and heard: "If Ida just taken that damned kid fishing that day."

His sentence trailed off without an answer to how life would be different, but everyone knew. Someone muttered some reassurance, but all I heard was my father's remorse.

How was it he could love other children so much and not us?

WALLS OF ANGER

School became my escape, and my friends were quintessential. When I was away from home, I could pretend it was a normal place. I never talked to any of my friends about my home life. I was too afraid they would judge me for the behaviors of my father. The apple doesn't fall far from the tree, you know. I never actually lied about my home life. I just became good at skirting the questions I didn't want to answer ... up until I had some friends stay over.

I'd begged out of hosting sleepovers for years, but I'd been to my friends' houses so many times and none of them had ever been to mine. Dad hadn't been violent for several months, so I took a gamble.

The night of my slumber party went great. Dad was gone. I wished for the millionth time he'd just stay away forever. Around midnight, my friends and I settled into sleeping bags around my room and soon fell asleep. Sometime in the middle of the night I awoke to a commotion downstairs. I prayed it would end before my friends heard.

It didn't.

One by one, they sat up with wide eyes and asked me what was going on.

I was used to straining my ears for the details of conversations below. I knew tonight's noises weren't angry sounds. They were the sounds of a room filled with drunks. Dad had come bursting into the house with a group of friends he'd invited home from the bar. I didn't recognize any of the voices except my father's and one other—my sister's husband.

I could see the terror in my friends' eyes and realized how foreign everything must be to them. No one came home drunk in the middle of the night at their houses, and I had no idea how to explain what was happening in mine. I decided to only tell half of the truth.

I told my friends it was my sister's husband and his friends. Visible relief washed over their faces ... until we heard the footsteps on the stairs. The unknown intruder's ascent was slow with intermittent loud thumps when he fell against the wall of the stairwell. There was nothing upstairs except Mark's and my bedrooms.

My friends crouched together in the corner of my room. I tried to tell them it was just my sister's husband. He was probably just coming up to her old room to get something.

The truth was, I wasn't sure of anything.

I grabbed the tennis racquet from its usual place in the corner and went to the closed door of my room. I pressed my ear against it, as if I hadn't been listening intently all along. Mostly, I was trying to look like I didn't have experience in things like that. I had to at least pretend it wasn't a regular occurrence.

The footsteps stopped in my brother's room.

The doors of our old house creaked as much as the stairs, and the knobs were sturdy old porcelain things that clicked when the mechanism caught or released. I turned the knob slowly to make sure nothing had a chance to clank. When the stopper released, I opened the door just enough to see into my brother's room. Whoever had come upstairs was standing directly over my baby brother's bed. The man was rubbing my sleeping brother's head.

The courage I'd never had when the perpetrator was my father flooded my body as I looked at this stranger. I didn't care if the door creaked. I burst through it with the tennis racquet raised above my head.

"Get away from my brother!" I demanded.

I no longer cared that my friends might be listening. I walked toward the stranger who was raising his hands and walking backward away from my brother's bed. He started to explain how he was just looking at the boy and how he was a friend of dad's.

I didn't care.

I'm sure the man must have thought I was certifiably insane as I stalked toward him with my racquet ready to strike. I didn't care about that either. He backed away until he reached the stairwell, then he turned and raced back down the stairs. The drunken awkwardness he had on the way up was replaced by fear as he effortlessly bounded down two steps at a time.

The stranger was gone and that was all that mattered.

As my friends drifted off to restless sleep, I prayed for my father's death. I was angry with him, with his stupid drunken friends, with my sister—but mostly I was angry with myself. My school and home life should never have crossed paths. I would make sure they never did again.

***

I joined every group, sport, and extracurricular activity offered by the little town where we lived. If it could get me out of my house, I would be more than willing to sign up. It may have served me better if a little of my escape had included study groups. It didn't.

In grade school, English had been my favorite subject. It was mostly about memorizing the meanings of words, learning how to spell them, and learning how to put them together to make sentences. I'd been doing that since Mom started reading to me. I could get good grades with hardly any effort, so that's all I ever put into it.

High school brought a different kind of English class than I'd ever experienced. We discussed literature and had a chance to do our own creative writing. We didn't have to just answer questions about something we read; we had to think about it.

I was used to being told to shut up, but now we were being asked to speak up. No one had ever wanted my opinions, and I was positive no one would want to know about my feelings.

In our first poetry assignment we were to come up with something that rhymed. I thought about the brilliance of my *Dr. Seuss Sleep Book* and knew I could never come up with anything like that. I expected my paper to come back with a great big "STUPID!!" written across the top of the page. It didn't. When the teacher handed me my paper, it had A+ in big red letters across the top. And next to the grade were handwritten comments. No one had ever taken the time to write positive comments on my homework before.

I couldn't wait until the next assignment and the feedback that followed. Good, bad, or indifferent, at least I didn't have to guess what the teacher thought of my work. Negative comments always included a suggestion about what I could have done differently. That meant there was hope for me!

When there was something that I needed to improve, the teacher explained it to me without calling me names or raising her voice. When there was something I did well, she placed the credit squarely on my shoulders. Her name was Miss Herrick, and she was the first teacher to look at me and say, "I think you could be somebody."

She became the confidante of my soul.

I wrote poems that talked about sunshine, flowers, serial killing, and demonic possession. She never called Child Protective Services to notify the authorities of an up-and-coming mass murderer. She never worried about me plotting against the world. She took my writings for exactly what they were ... stories. She praised my creativity, developed my understanding of the English language, and most importantly ... she kept my secrets!

Miss Herrick kept the secret that I felt left out. She kept the secret that my father beat my mother. She never told anyone who I was in love with or who'd made me mad, and she never used my words against me. When she asked if she could read aloud something I'd written in class, I felt like the next Shakespeare. She believed in me! She told me she was proud of me, and she wanted to see more of my work.

Miss Herrick's lack of judgmentalism enabled me to be truly candid for the first time in my life. More and more my stories contained information about real life and my struggle to understand injustices. Life was supposed to be fair, and my writing reflected my struggle to accept that it not only wasn't, but it also never would be.

My belief that life should be fair made it even harder to understand the life Mom was living.

Mom worked, either outside or inside the home, every moment she was awake. She never said a negative word against anyone, including dad, and she would give the shirt off her back to help someone in need. Our minister always said we were supposed to get what we gave, but all Mom gave was love, and all she received in return was crap. It didn't make sense. It wasn't fair.

The kindest person I knew, besides my mother, was my best friend Julie. We had been best friends since I moved to the school in second grade. If anyone knew my secrets, it was Julie; but she never brought up things I didn't want to talk about.

Toward the end of our sophomore year in high school, Julie confessed she had a crush on one of the boys in eleventh grade. I knew she was too shy to ever let him know how she felt. Of course I took it upon myself to hook them up. When he told me he felt the same way about her, I couldn't wait to tell her.

In the beginning of their relationship, I was the matchmaking hero who had fixed them up, but it wasn't long before I became the third wheel. As the two of them spent more time together, she and I spent less. I missed her.

Of course, admitting that I missed my friend would make me vulnerable and that, to me, was unacceptable. Instead, I fell back into the safety net of hate and blamed my friend's boyfriend for ruining our relationship. When she didn't immediately dump him to salvage our friendship, I decided she must not care about me after all. I stopped talking to her at school and stopped taking her calls at home. If she spoke to me in class, I pretended not to hear. When she tried to talk to me in the hallways, I acted like she was invisible.

By the time we started our junior year we had both moved on to other friends, which only proved to me again how little she cared. Oh sure, she still tried to talk to me, but it was too little too late. She'd made her choice and I'd made mine.

The truth was, she had done absolutely nothing to warrant the treatment I gave her.

The only thing worse than losing my friend would have been to admit that I deserved to lose her. If I'd been honest with myself, I would have realized sooner that I didn't deserve her friendship. Despite the hateful things I put her through, she never once said a bad word about me in return. I didn't deserve her kindness. I deserved her hatred, but she didn't have a stockpile of animosity built up like I did.

She wasn't a monster like I was, and she hadn't built walls of anger.

DOMESTIC VIOLENCE LIVES AMONG US

The first time I ever heard the term domestic violence was in sociology class. It had never occurred to me that what happened in our house might be happening to other families. It blew my mind to realize we weren't the only people walking on eggshells.

Dad and I had always had an unwritten agreement to just stay out of each other's way. Unless we absolutely needed to talk to each other, we just ignored each other's existence. Of course, that didn't make me exempt from his lectures.

"Stay away from that!" he said every time I went near the tree that held his deer stringing invention. "Don't you go swinging on that," he'd say. But he wasn't home a lot, and one day I made a decision.

"I'm gonna swing on that."

Dad had taken an old oxbow and tied a huge metal pulley to the bottom. One day after hunting, he and a group of three friends decided to finally hang it in a tree. It took them about a hundred attempts to throw the end of the rope over a branch none of them could reach, but eventually they accomplished it. Three of the guys lifted the contraption up so another guy could tie it up into the tree. Once it was secured in place, dad attached a hook to the end of his thick pulley rope. They stuck the hook through the deer they had killed and used the pulley to hoist it into the air. I never understood why hanging meat outside where the flies landed on it for three days was a good thing, but apparently it is.

No deer had been on the oxbow for weeks, but the hoisting contraption was set up. The ends of the oxbow would make great handles. Clearly if it could hold the weight of a deer, it could hold me.

I crouched down directly below the pulley, then used my legs to launch myself as high as I possibly could. Feeling like an acrobat, I reached both arms out wide and grabbed the handles of the oxbow.

My moment of victory was interrupted by a crack from the branch above my head. Everything else happened in an instant as the branch, oxbow, and ten-inch steel pully crashed down onto me. A stinging sensation burned at the top of my head, but mostly I felt fuzzy. I was on my knees with my back bent to the ground, but the contraption had landed in front of me. When the fuzziness started to fade, I realized what had just happened. I was in trouble.

I sat up straight but still on my knees and looked down at my white sweater. It was turning red from the top down in an almost perfect line of movement.

"Whoa, that affected my eyesight."

That was the moment I put my hand to the top of my head. When I pulled my hand back, my entire palm and all my fingers were covered in blood. Oh man, I was in *big* trouble. Getting to my feet and running into the house was mostly instinctual, and the fact that Mom was home was pure luck. She was standing at the kitchen sink when she saw the goriest sight imaginable. There I stood, my shirt now dripping blood from the bottom hem.

"Oh my God," was Mom's immediate reaction as she reached for the drawer and grabbed a towel. "Sit down at the table. Let me see." Mom guided me to the closest chair and told me to put my head down. The next thing I knew, Mom was pushing down hard on the spot that was really starting to hurt.

"Diane, get in here!" Mom yelled. "I need your help!" The sense of urgency in her voice was obvious, and Diane didn't need the usual second plea. Within seconds she was in the kitchen.

"Hold this towel down as hard as you can," Mom instructed. "I have to call the doctor to see what to do."

The doctor walked Mom through stopping the bleeding, which wasn't much more than she was already doing. After she hung up the phone, Mom asked Diane to keep holding the towel. "I think I'm going to throw up," Mom said as she stretched out on the cold linoleum.

At that point, Diane couldn't resist a peek. I felt her peel the towel away from my head, but I wasn't expecting her exclamation. "Ewww, I can see brains."

As my mother and sister worked to stop my bleeding and nurse my wound, all I could think about was how much trouble I was going to be in.

"Why don't we go to town?" I asked. "We could go to town and do this," I said. "We could just hold this against my head in the car." I pleaded, but nothing I said was going to get my mother to move me. I was stuck in my position with my head down on my arms at the kitchen table, knowing I was going to die.

He's going to kill me," I thought repeatedly.

I still had my head down, but a bag of ice had been added to the towel pressed against my head when I heard the car pull up to the garage.

I was as good as dead.

Time slowed to nothing but my heart beat at three times its normal cadence. At any moment my father was going to walk through the kitchen door and kill me. I heard the door open.

There had to have been a significant trail of blood leading into the house and, of course, his deer stringing invention was lying on the ground. He didn't say anything at all, which made my heart beat even faster.

"Move outta the way," dad said to Diane as he took over the towel and ice bag duty. I felt him lift the towel from my head; then I could feel him inspecting my injury.

Just kill me already.

When he saw what he needed to see, dad laid the towel filled with ice back on my wound and patted it once. The pain in my head had become increasingly worse since the accident, so patting anything against my wound felt like lighting a fire in my brain. Then he walked out of the room.

He didn't kill me!

I didn't even get in any trouble! Amazed at my good fortune, I could finally think about what had occurred.

My hair was caked with blood in various stages of drying. Mom had described the wound to the doctor and his response had been: "Doesn't sound like there's much to stitch up. Just keep an eye on her and let me know if she starts to feel sick."

Though I didn't feel sick, I was exhausted. The stress of what my father might do when he found me disobeying him had taken everything out of me. I fell asleep on the table. The next thing I knew, Mom was waking me up so she could set the table for dinner.

We didn't have a shower, only a bathtub, so I washed my hair in the kitchen sink while Mom set the table. I was shocked at the amount of blood my hair could hold, and my head throbbed when I bent over to lower it into the sink.

Eventually the wound healed, but the question I had would linger forever. *Why was I so terrified of my father's reaction?* Most of the time his threats were empty because he never followed through, but then every so often ... he did.

I became enthralled by the topic of domestic violence, believing other people's experiences might somehow help me make sense of my own.

Then my sociology teacher said something that stopped my heart: "Kids who grow up in an abusive household will grow up to abuse their own children."

Could that really be? Was I doomed?

I needed to learn more, but I couldn't ask my sociology teacher. If I did, he would know what was happening in my household. He would know I was just a piece of white trash who wasn't worth his time.

I'd have to research the subject on my own. Then the answer fell right in my lap. We were required to write term papers for our senior year; my topic would be child abuse.

Our school library had only a few books on child abuse, and they were all written from an academic standpoint. I wanted to know real stories about real people.

The teacher had suggested we go to the University library twenty miles away and had even arranged special passes for us to check out material without being college students. My best friend had a car, so a group of us carpooled twenty miles to campus.

I'm not sure what I expected to find, but the stories were far worse than anything I'd ever imagined. One of the books talked about a little girl who had reached up while her father was cooking and almost burned herself. As punishment, her father held her little hand over the open flame for one minute. The book showed a picture of the little girl's charred, fingerless hand rippled with scars.

Another story I read still haunts me to this day. A father was so angry with his daughter for wetting her pants that he flung a cast iron skillet at her. The pan hit her little head hard enough to knock the top section of her skull off. Her brother and sisters watched the entire event, helpless. They watched as she died with half of her brain splattered across their kitchen floor. After their father buried her in the backyard, they could say nothing of her existence.

The world forgot about the little girl, but her siblings never did. Her older brother was so traumatized by the event that he fell into a catatonic state which ultimately landed him in an asylum.

The father who'd murdered his daughter was never arrested. The only witnesses were either too afraid to talk about it or unable to speak at all. It was more than twenty years after the little girl died that her story was told—through her catatonic brother.

A new psychiatrist had decided to tackle the mysterious case of the boy who seemed physically fine but refused to do anything except stare at the wall. The boy had been spoon-fed since his arrival decades earlier, and pureed baby food was all he ate. The doctor decided a good way to bond with the silent man would be to give him a treat. Rather than his normal jars of baby food, she brought a plate of spaghetti into the boy's room. When the doctor set the plate on his tray, the boy screamed hysterically and struggled to get as far from the plate as possible. His catatonic state was over, and eventually the truth came out. The spaghetti, he confessed, looked like brains.

Life wasn't fair for that little boy or his siblings. But it also wasn't fair to the father, who had died years earlier without ever having paid for what he'd done.

The books I checked out went on and on with stories of one sadistic monster after another. In some cases, the parents were sentenced to prison—but the child was still dead. In other cases, there were horrific events that children lived through, only to suffer with scars and fears that haunted them the rest of their lives.

None of it was fair, and none of the victims could be made whole again.

Even stepping in and physically saving them didn't result in fairness because the damage was done. The only fair thing would be to turn back time and erase the entire event ... or require a screening test for prospective parents. If they had pre-destined abusive tendencies, they'd be disqualified. Of course, wouldn't that then disqualify me?

I sobbed as I read some of the stories and imagined how scared the children must have been. At the end of all my research, I realized something I wasn't expecting. I didn't have it so bad.

Mom certainly had some stories that would put her in the ranks of the books I read, but personally, I could have had things much worse.

So, my dad hated me. Big deal. I hated him right back.

As I worked through my anger and shock over the mountain of abuse cases I'd read, I wrote poems and short stories about my feelings. Miss Herrick read them all. She read poems she hadn't assigned and stories she never asked me to write. She would even meet with me after school to talk about them.

Miss Herrick never yelled at me or called me names, and I loved hearing her opinions. She didn't always love everything I wrote, but she always loved that I wrote it.

Like too many young talented teachers, she was recruited away from our small-town school too soon. The new English teacher was the girls' basketball coach, and I don't think literature was his first choice of subjects. Unfortunately, small-town coaches don't have the luxury of specializing exclusively in sports. If he wanted to make a living, he had to teach the subjects that were offered to him. Thrilled or not, he was there ... teaching literature.

One of the works we studied was Shakespeare's *Hamlet*. The teacher asked if anyone wanted to explain a particular character's motivation and I, of course, raised my hand. After I gave what I believed to be a particularly brilliant summary, the teacher/coach looked at me, pointed his finger at me, and said, "Wrong! Anyone else?"

Clearly, he did not see the budding genius Miss Herrick had seen.

I suppose I could have chosen to let him take away the confidence she had ignited in me. Instead, I wondered, *"How the heck did he know? Did he ever meet Shakespeare?"*

While sulking about my rejection, I suddenly realized something. If having just one person believe in me made me feel like I mattered in life, maybe that one person could be me. The basketball coach may have embarrassed me, but he didn't break me. I decided then and there that no one could ever break me again. If I didn't let myself care about anyone too much, they would never have the power to hurt me. And if any of them hurt the people I did care about, God help them.

My anger about domestic violence was no longer just about my own father, but about all the parents I read about who hurt their children. In my mind, they were all worthless pieces of trash who added nothing but grief to the world.

The world would be better off without them.

GLUTTON FOR PUNISHMENT

My seventeenth birthday arrived during a winter storm as always. Mom was still prepared with a cake. Dad was present because we were snowed in.

As Mom said, "Okay, you have to blow out the candles," I thought about what normal teenagers probably wished for: a car, designer clothes, a boyfriend.

I wished my father would die.

It was the same wish I'd made since I first started blowing out candles. I hated my father more than anything in the world, and I wanted him out of our lives, preferably in the most painful way possible. I opened my birthday presents—none of which I remember now—as my mom, sister, and brother sat around the table. It wasn't unusual for dad not to join us, even if he was in the house. He rarely participated in family activities, unless they revolved around him and his friends. While the rest of us were in the kitchen, dad was in the living room doing something I couldn't care less about.

Then, out of nowhere, he came into the kitchen and handed me a present. He had never given me a present before in my life. He had never even known when my birthday was! And yet, there he stood with a package he had wrapped himself. He had bought me a gift. He knew it was my birthday.

I opened the package to find a baby blue comb/brush combo that operated like a pocketknife. It was long like a ruler with a comb on one side and a brush on the other. The two sides folded together so it could be easily carried in a purse or a back pocket. I always kept a comb in my back pocket! I was known for it at the roller-skating rink. My father knew something about me!

I had to remind myself I didn't care, but he had never given me anything before. I tried to remind myself I hated his guts, but he picked it out by himself. He had thought of me. Why was it so difficult for me to hold onto my hatred of him? He deserved to be hated! Why did feelings of love and sadness for him leak through the wall around my heart?

After my party, I carefully put the gift on my dresser with no intention of ever touching it again. It was just a stupid comb set. It probably didn't even cost five dollars.

Why did I keep going back to look at it more closely? Why did I keep folding and unfolding it again and again like it was magical?

A few days after my birthday, I came home from school and found the family dog chewing on my baby blue brush/comb set. I had been looking at it when I left for school and left it on my bed by mistake. My pocket comb set was covered in bite marks, and the two sides no longer folded together. I yelled at my dog—my best friend—as I took the mangled blue plastic out of her mouth. I held the brush and tried to close it, but it was broken and would never be the same. I sat down next to my dog and sobbed. My comb set—that I couldn't care less about—was ruined. The only gift I had ever received from my father, the person I hated most in the world, was destroyed. Why was I heartbroken? I had never been more confused in my life.

I placed the chewed item carefully in my dresser drawer where it would be safe from future canine attacks, still wondering why it mattered to me so much. Why couldn't I just throw it away? I should just hate it. Why did it matter that dad had picked it out and wrapped it personally just for me? I should just hate him the way he deserved to be hated. How could I want someone who mattered so little in my life to care about me? I reminded myself I didn't. Caring would only mean he could hurt me again, and I would never let that happen.

With the comb set out of sight, it would surely be out of mind. But I didn't stop thinking about it, and I never stopped asking myself why.

As childhood began fading into adult hood, Traci and I were able to drive ourselves wherever we wanted to go. Well, she could. I didn't have a car. There was never a question where we would go; it was always to the nearby college town where the guys from the roller rink lived.

My Saturday night romance with Tim had been in the same phase for years, until one weekend when my family was going hunting.

My high school band had a marching competition on Saturday. As a member of the band, I was required to be there, but my family had plans to go on a hunting trip. Easy solution: they gave me a set of keys and said, "Make sure you get up on time tomorrow." Mom walked out the door to load the last bit of baggage in the car.

As my family drove out of the driveway, I was already on the phone with Traci. We went to the roller-skating rink as usual, but after we left there, we decided to cruise Main Street. Tim was aware of our plan and knew I had no curfew for the evening. He promised that after he clocked out, he would find us on Main. My heart raced at the idea of spending time alone with him.

By the time we met up with Tim, Pete, and their friend Brent on Main Street it was time for Traci to go home. Tim and I planned to meet at a park on the other end of Main, Pete gave Traci a ride home.

My heart had never beat faster than it did when I climbed into the passenger side of Tim's pickup. We talked, kissed, and smoked cigarettes as we listened to the radio. "Arthur's Theme" by Christopher Cross was the number one song and played over and over throughout the night. By the light of the 7-11 across the street,

I fell even more in love with Tim than I'd ever been. Our amorous kissing never led to anything further, but that didn't matter. Neither of us made any moves to take things further. It was enough just to be in each other's arms.

When the radio announcer said it was 5:00 a.m., I knew it was time to leave. I had to be at school by 6:00 a.m. to catch the band bus, and it was a thirty-minute drive if I didn't stop home first. By the time we'd said our final goodbye and had our final kiss, there was no chance I would be able to stop at home.

With my hair messed up and two significant hickeys on my neck, I entered the high school locker room to change into my uniform.

"What happened?" Traci asked. "Are you just getting home?"

By then several girls had gathered around us at the mirror, looking at my hickeys and giving advice on how to cover them up.

I could barely wait to tell Traci every detail of the story on the bus.

Surely my true love and I would have an actual relationship after that night—but nothing changed. He was never on the other end of a ringing telephone. He never asked me out on a date. He still asked me to couple's skate, but we never spoke of the night in the park.

When I heard he was going to prom with a girl from my town my heart shattered into a million pieces, each stabbing into my chest simultaneously. My pain wasn't just the result of my broken heart; it was also the pain of my gullibility. I had fallen for Tim's charm a million times with no reason to expect anything between us to change. Even so, my epiphany flew out the window the next time I saw Tim's smile and bright blue eyes gazing my direction. I was a glutton for punishment.

Was that why Mom stayed with dad?

I'LL DRINK TO THAT

By the middle of our junior year, I had apologized to Julie at least ten times. Our two friend groups had merged into a diverse collection of personalities where everyone contributed something to our eclectic clique. We had sports stars, brainiacs, beauty queens, and me. At best, I could be described as average, but even that relied on the generosity of the individual doing the evaluation. The only uniqueness I could contribute to the group was my sarcastic wit, which was generally more biting than humorous.

Spring cheerleading tryouts were being held and a few of my friends and I decided to try out. I'd been selected the previous year for the girls' basketball cheer squad, but I opted to play on the team instead. The year before that I wasn't selected. The tryouts would be my last chance to be a high school cheerleader, and I wanted to be chosen.

I created a unique cheer with the help of a seasoned cheerleader from another town and scored well enough to be in the top three candidates! Being in the top three meant that I had first choice of the squads I wanted to be on. First choice was always football because homecoming happened during football season. Second choice was always boys' basketball. I wanted to be a boys' basketball cheerleader. They did harder cheers, cooler stunts, and dated the starting players. Each one of them was a "White Pants Person." I wasn't. I knew I wasn't good enough to be part of their team. Even with hours of practice, I just didn't have the coordination to do cheers that involved arms and legs working together.

I also wasn't good enough to think I belonged with the other girls. I'd heard that from Grandma Naomi all my life. In fact, I heard it again when I went to her house after school on the day of cheerleading tryouts. I was excited to tell her my news and started right in.

"We had cheerleading tryouts today and …"

"Take your shoes off." Grandma Naomi's voice was irritated, and I'd already taken my shoes off when I came in. She continued, "I don't know why you even bother with things like that. They're never going to pick you because you don't have the right last name. You're just setting yourself up for disappointment, so don't come crying to me when you don't make it."

"I made it," I replied in a flat voice.

"Oh, that's great! Good for you" were the words I heard as I walked away to wait for Mom in Grandma's living room.

She wasn't supposed to be part of my family anymore anyway. Why did her opinion still affect how I felt? My feelings of accomplishment and excitement about my senior year were completely dashed by a couple sentences from her mouth.

I hated the fact that she continued to have so much power over me.

***

In the spring of my junior year in high school, Mark and I came home to find Mom standing in the middle of the driveway.

"Mark, I put a snack on the table for you. Go on in and set your books down." I watched as my little brother skipped to the front door of our house. I had to be in serious trouble if Mom not only had to talk to me alone, but outside. I wracked my brain to think of something I had done, but nothing came to mind.

"I need to tell you something," Mom said in an ominous tone. By the look on her face, it was going to be bad.

I swallowed hard and prepared for the worst.

Mom studied my expression to gauge my mood and nervously told me her news. "I filed paperwork to divorce your father this afternoon."

"What?" My eyes flew open wide. "Are you serious?" It was a good thing Mom told me the news outside because I screamed and jumped all around like a lunatic. It wasn't bad news. It was the absolute best possible news I could have ever received! It was finally the answer to my prayers!

It took dad about a month to move out of the house, but the wind was out of his sails and his fury didn't mean much to me at that point. He was an unwelcome guest in a place he no longer belonged.

Dad's mother was beside herself at the idea that her family could be embroiled in a divorce. It was 1983 in a town of less than 2,000 people. Divorce was uncommon and generally a scandalous thing only pursued by "women's libbers."

Grandma couldn't accept the fact that Mom's decision to divorce dad could be based on anything her precious son had done. She convinced herself there had to have been some outside influence corrupting Mom's choices. Since Grandma hated me anyway, she reached the conclusion it was I who talked Mom into kicking dad out of our house and filing for divorce.

In the beginning I didn't really care what Grandma thought, it even made me laugh. I was just elated that our nightmare was ending. I had no idea what lengths my grandmother would go to in protecting her son's reputation. Grandma told anyone in town who would listen that I had a drinking problem, and dad just couldn't stay there and "watch her destroy the family he loves with all his heart."

I consoled myself with the fact that Grandma's friends knew dad well enough to know he spent his days in the local bar. They also knew I was involved in every school activity and had never even been grounded. Well, not since we moved to Arlington anyway.

As the host of her daily coffee hour, Grandma was able to add more details to her ever-evolving story. "He just can't condone that girl's affair with a married man." She said it in a way that seemed like it saddened her to the core. Grandma claimed she saw me get out of the married man's pickup truck one night when I was supposed to be at a church function. Grandma lived across from the church and pointed out I wouldn't have needed a ride if I'd been at the church like I said. There were enough elements of truth in her story that, suddenly, her ridiculous accusations had everyone in town looking at me sideways.

The married man she was talking about was the minister of my church, and he did drop me off at her house on the night I told Mom I was going to a church event. What Grandma either left out or didn't know, was that our entire Luther League group had gone roller-skating twenty miles away on that cold winter night. The minister had a pickup truck with a topper on the back, so I, along with about ten other Luther League members, rode in the topper while the minister and his wife rode in the cab of the pickup. Mom was to pick me up at Grandma's house, so that's where the minister and his wife dropped me off when we came home from skating. Yes, the minister and his wife could have just dropped us all off at the church, but they knew it was cold, and they didn't want us walking even a short distance with our skates and bags.

When the minister stopped his truck in front of my grandparents' house, I crawled out of the back and walked up to the driver's side window. The minister rolled it down, and I thanked him and his wife for taking us skating.

In Grandma's version of the story, she left out the pastor's wife sitting in the passenger seat. She left out my classmates, still in the back of the truck, who were also being dropped off at their homes. My grandmother morphed my "thank you" to a pastor and his wife into me saying goodbye to my lover. She always included just enough of the truth to make her stories believable.

The extra details that Grandma added into her story didn't matter in her mind. By leaving out just a few of the key points, Grandma could wholeheartedly end her story with, "And that's the God's honest truth." And it was ... from her perspective.

She'd told the stories to all her friends in our tiny town. Her friends were the parents of kids I went to school with. I was mortified and completely powerless to defend my reputation. Would the minister and his wife find out about Grandma's gossip? Would the kids in the back of the truck?

I was mortified.

I'd accepted the fact that dad and Grandma hated my guts through years of their pretending I didn't exist. But to take an active role in destroying me? This was a new low even for Grandma.

There were ten other kids in the truck topper that night. They could back up every single thing I said. But they weren't supposed to know anything about my crazy life. What if I asked them to stand up for me and they hadn't heard the rumor? I would just be making it worse. There were sideways looks and people who stared at me a little too long when I walked down the street, but no one had the courage to ask me directly about what they had heard.

Mom knew the truth. My entire church knew the truth! The youth outing had been on the church calendar for crying out loud! That didn't change the fact people were looking at me funny.

"Don't worry about what she says," Mom assured me. "Everyone knows Grandma just makes stories up, and if anyone believes it, they obviously don't know you."

So, I was to just ignore them. Once again, I stood alone against the world.

There may have been only a few people who believed Grandma's lies, but they would retell the story to their families who would retell it to their families … and each new storyteller would add their own embellishments.

Certainly, Grandma's friends knew her well enough to know she was lying, and it wasn't long before the story died out. But why didn't anyone have the courage to stand up to her? She was just a tiny woman in stature, but no one wanted to be on her bad side.

At least Grandma was only focused on hurting *me*. She never told anyone who the "married man" was, because she "wasn't the kind of person who'd be gossiping about something like that." In truth, if they knew it was our pastor they would automatically know she was lying. Our pastor was the pillar of morality. But her friends didn't know which pastor from which town, so they had no real information to refute her story.

I tried to pretend my crazy grandmother's stories didn't hurt me, but they did. How could she dislike me so very much that she would be willing to make up complete lies? Even if no one came to my defense, I was confident someone would at least step up and defend the pastor. If only Grandma would slip up and tell her friends which pastor she saw. But she didn't. And still my mother's advice was to take the high road. I followed her advice and remained silent.

When Grandma added a new twist to her story, I thought for sure everyone would finally call bullshit. If they couldn't defend my morals, certainly they would argue my stupidity. Grandma started telling everyone who would listen that I personally drew up my parents' divorce papers.

I was only seventeen years old; and more importantly, I wasn't a prodigy in anything. Even the people who despised me couldn't possibly believe I would be smart enough to draft a divorce agreement. But the gossipmongers listened without filtering Grandma's words through logic. They listened, they embellished, and they repeated the story to their own circle of friends.

In my opinion, remaining silent was the same as agreeing. Even people who could defend me in private weren't comfortable being seen with me in a public setting. The public shunning may not have lasted long, but it was hard to get over the memory of how many people turned their backs in judgment on me.

I began to believe it didn't matter what I did. My sociology teacher was right. Regardless of what I did or said, I was a loser either way.

Why wasn't I worth defending?

What difference did it make if I had morals or not? I would to be judged guilty either way, so I might as well start deserving the verdict. If nothing else, deviant behavior might get me some attention.

I decided to start out by making good on the drinking problem.

CRY FOR HELP

Traci had an older brother who was willing to take us to the bars. Our favorite was called the Lucky Lady. If we arrived at the bar before 6:30 p.m., when the bouncers started work, we were free and clear. They never went around to card people who were already in the bar.

If we had a late start, Traci's brother Steve just bought beer and we all went road tripping.

One night Steve brought a new girlfriend along. She was from Washington, D.C. and spent the entire night talking about how sheltered and backward everyone from South Dakota was. Doing my best impersonation of a "bad ass," I tried to defend the worthiness of my entire state. Then she showed me the round scars up and down her arm.

"I got these from playing Chicken," she bragged as she rolled up each sleeve of her sweater. "No one in South Dakota probably even knows what Chicken is." She pushed one of her sleeves back down into place. "Even if they did, no one here would have the guts to play it."

"I have guts," I said out loud. Truth be told, I had no idea what the game of Chicken was, but I was drunk ... and bullet proof.

Just because she lived in the city, it didn't mean she had anything on me. I'd lived in cities— granted when I was four—but I'd also lived in remote areas where no one could hear you scream. If she thought she had some worldly experience to lord over me, she could bring it on.

The girlfriend pushed her arm against mine and dropped her lit cigarette where our arms met. I might not be able to beat someone in a game of skill or intelligence, but I could certainly win a contest of pain.

To be honest, it hurt a lot more than I thought it would.

At first it was a biting sting, then it grew in intensity until it felt like my entire forearm was on fire. I wanted to pull my arm back and tell her what a stupid game it was, but chickening out would mean her stereotypes were correct. I couldn't let that happen. I would suffer through the pain silently. I gritted my teeth together as hard as I could and tried to think of anything other than the burning pain in my arm. After about two minutes, it didn't hurt anymore.

Ha! I could sit like that all day. In hindsight, the removal of the pain had nothing to do with my tolerance, strength, or commitment. The cigarette had burned away the nerves as it burned through my arm.

Eventually the cigarette burned itself out and we called it a draw. In the end, she had to admit I could take it as well as she could.

I'd won the respect of a person I'd never meet again with a scar I'd carry the rest of my life.

Regardless of how tough I tried to be on the weekends, my busy calendar kept weekdays flying. Even though the friends I partied with were the same friends I cheered with, played ball with, and learned to cook with, we were all well-behaved at school. It wasn't just because schools still allowed teachers to hit students back then. School was where we could make something of ourselves, and I wanted to fit in with my peers.

As my weekend behavior deteriorated, I never tried to hide what I was doing. More than anything else in the world, I wanted someone to care enough about me to stop my self-destruction. Yell at me, ground me, tell me I was worthless—anything would be better than pretending I didn't exist.

My sister was married with a newborn baby, my mother was newly single, and my father had moved away to a place I'd never been invited to see. Mark had his own friend group, and they were at the age where they began hanging out together after school. My refuge became school, and my friends became my saviors.

I became their corruptor.

I passed all my classes, and I was in every activity the school offered. I didn't yell and scream at my mother like Diane had done when she was a teenager. I didn't even prod my father into explosions like my sister had done when she lived at home. No one had to worry about what I was doing, so they didn't.

One night when I came home from drinking, Mom told me to give the cat some milk. I knew I wasn't walking very well, and I certainly couldn't form a coherent sentence. I had drunk the equivalent of four bottles of wine.

After getting the carton of milk from the refrigerator, I struggled to open the spout. As I fumbled with the milk, I sputtered some incoherent things about how I was all alone. Grandma was still telling people terrible things about me, and no one cared if I lived or died.

I was still rambling as I opened the spout and poured milk into the cat's bowl. I didn't bend over. I didn't pick up the bowl. I just poured it from standing up and milk splashed everywhere.

"Just go to bed," Mom said, exasperated. She knew I was drunk. Surely, we would have some kind of conversation the next day about my behavior.

We didn't.

Mom confided in my sister that she couldn't bring it up to me because she was the one who had brought the alcohol. The event was a "Bring Your Own Booze" concert, and Mom had done just that—she brought a duffle bag of bottles to choose from during the concert. It seemed like she was trying to impress my father, but why would that be? She was divorcing him.

Those were my thoughts when I snuck the first bottle of wine from Mom's bag.

Dad seemed to be using his connections to the band to win Mom's affections back. He sat in with the band, of course, and sang songs he dedicated to "the woman who made everything wonderful in my life possible."

I wanted to vomit at the sight of the two of them swooning. I was appalled that after everything it took to get away from dad, there was now a chance it was all going to be for nothing. When no one was looking, I took another bottle out of the bag and sat far enough behind my mother so she wouldn't notice me.

After I finished the second bottle, I took another one out of the bag, and I drank it.

Mom must not have been drinking very much because she drove us home. I rambled on about Grandma's hateful lies for most of the half hour drive while Mom silently kept her hands on the wheel and eyes on the road.

Even as drunk as I was, I could tell Mom was exasperated with me even before I gave the cat milk. She had every right to be. I was sure Mom would finally talk to me about what was going on and why I didn't fit in anywhere.

She didn't.

I hated my grandmother, and I wanted Mom to hate her too. I had watched again and again as Grandma intentionally hurt both Mom and me.

Why did I have to be nice to someone who wasn't nice to me? For the few moments I had lain in bed before passing out, I thought about my mother choosing my grandmother over me.

On the outside I was a mediocre athlete, saxophone player, cheerleader, letterman, and an active participant in FHA, A-Club, Pep Club, Yearbook Staff, and a background character in most every play my high school performed.

On the inside, all I ever wanted was to be someone else. The perfect life I had thought would fall into place when dad was out of the picture wasn't happening.

I realized I'd been wishing for the wrong person's death. *I* was the person the world would be better off without.

That wasn't the first time I'd thought about ending my life, and it wouldn't be the last. I had secret notebooks with versions of suicide notes I'd written to various people I loved. No one ever knew it was something I thought about, and I never planned an attempt. Sometimes it just seemed like an easy way to get out of the crap I didn't want to deal with in life.

***

Then—for once—my worst fear did *not* come true. My parents did *not* reconcile, and my father did *not* move back into our house.

Aside from Grandma's continued antics, things had been leagues better since dad moved out. It started to seem like we might be a normal family for once, even if we were the products of a broken home. Perhaps my prayers *were* being answered.

DÉJÀ VU

Near the end of my senior year my father's landlord died and the man's kids sold the property almost immediately. Dad was homeless. Personally, I didn't see how that was our problem. Dad's parents had an extra bedroom he could move into. Or he could always stay with one of his girlfriends.

But Mom wasn't the spiteful person I was. She told dad he could stay with us until he found somewhere else to live.

From the second he brought his box of meager belongings through the door he acted like he owned the place. Mom even seemed glad to have him there and was grateful when he started pitching in around the house. She saw his efforts to fix the things he'd never gotten around to when they were married as helpful. I saw them as overstepping his bounds. At dinner time I fumed that he had the gall to sit at the head of the table. He acted like it was still his place. My mother and brother thought it meant nothing more than a place to sit and that I shouldn't worry about it.

But I saw our entire family dynamic regressing. Even if I had been acting up, I liked it when it was just Mom, my brother, and me sitting across from each other and talking about our days. With dad sitting at the head of the table, we all had to turn to look at him. He engaged Mom in more conversation than they'd had the entire time they were married. He was suddenly interested in everything she had to say and even complimented her regularly.

It didn't matter if he convinced the whole world he was a changed man. He had stolen the beginning of my childhood, and now he was back to steal the ending.

In my opinion, he was using Mom's kindness just like he'd always done, and it was infuriating that she couldn't see it. I saw the way she looked at him while they were talking. She still loved him, and he was going to convince her to reconcile.

I would be leaving for college in a few months so it really shouldn't have bothered me. Dad had always been kinder to my brother than he'd ever been to my sister or me. Maybe dad being back in the house would be a positive thing after I was gone.

But I knew better. Reconciliation between my parents would change everything. It didn't matter how nice he was being; he would eventually turn back into the monster I grew up with, and when he did my brother would be alone! Under no circumstance could I let that happen.

GOODBYES

On the day of my graduation, I worried dad would show up drunk and ruin my big day. As I lined up with my classmates at the back of the school gym, I searched the section where my mom, brother, sister, brother-in-law, niece, and both sets of grandparents sat. Dad wasn't there. Tardiness was never a good sign for him because it meant he was drinking. I searched the bleachers and the scattering of people still coming through the doors, but he was nowhere to be seen.

Good! Maybe he wouldn't show up. As I took my first step toward the stage, I wasn't near comfortable enough to make eye contact with the crowd. I stared at the floor in contemplation of each step I had to take in my new high heels. Mom stepped into the aisle to take a picture, so I saw the row where my family was seated—still no sign of my father.

Nobody would miss their own kid's graduation, would they?

When the ceremony was over, my classmates and I lined up on the front sidewalk of the building I'd known since second grade. We hugged each other and promised to keep in touch as our friends and relatives lined up to congratulate us.

I'd shaken hands with about 200 people by the time my family made their way to the line of graduates. My heart beat harder. Surely dad would have caught up to the rest of my family by then. *What would he say to me? What if he tried to hug me? How weird would that be?*

When Mom reached my place in the line, she took my hand in both of hers and said, "Your dad wanted to be here, but he had a fishing derby today."

I sucked in a breath too quickly and tears started filling my eyes.

In hindsight, there was no reason for me to expect him to be at my graduation. I just never imagined a person wouldn't *want* to see their child graduate. Regardless of the examples my brain brought forward to prove I was still just a glutton for punishment, my heart had wanted to believe he would be there.

As far as anyone in the crowd could tell, my tears were just an emotional moment with my mom—no different than any other graduate's reaction to seeing her mother—and yet mine were different.

The last summer of my youth was something I'd looked forward to all year long. Dad was still living with us and didn't seem interested in finding a new place. He would ruin my last summer of youth the same way he'd ruined everything else in my life.

Fortunately, I had a fulltime job that kept me away from the house all day. I'd taken a job as a farm hand at the local mink ranch. It was disgusting work, but it paid almost twice as much as any other job I could find. Plus, I had my nights and Sundays free.

I thought I had distanced myself enough that dad couldn't hurt me. Wrong again.

Upon arriving home after work one day, I discovered he had given my puppy to one of his drinking buddies.

"You're gonna go off to school and leave your mother to take care of that dog. It doesn't even know not to shit on the floor yet," he said as he pointed to a piece of dog feces on the floor, which he hadn't bothered to pick up. "And you're gonna put all that on your mom?"

He wasn't wrong. I could not find a reason my mother should take care of the puppy I brought home a month before leaving for college. But even if he was right, who the hell was he to speak for my mother?

As I fetched a paper towel from the kitchen and returned to the living room to pick up the dog poop, he continued chastising me.

"What are you gonna do if that dog wrecks something at the house while you're at work?" he asked pointedly.

"At least I could pay for it," I bit back at my father. I was proud of my jab as I walked away from him.

I'd gotten in a good one.

I'd beaten him just like I did that night on the stairs, and he deserved the dejected look I put on his face. He had no right to be a decision-maker in our home. He was an unwanted guest who constantly overstepped his bounds.

I wished he would just go back to where he came from and get out of my life.

While I may have acknowledged he was right on the inside, I had no intention of doing so on the outside. I held to my stance that he had no right to get rid of my puppy and used it to layer more hatred onto what I already felt for him.

If I could have been just a bit more honest with myself, it wasn't really the re-homing of my puppy that bothered me most. It bothered me that Mom must have confided in him that she didn't want the puppy to be there. She complained to him about me, while she stayed silent to me. He was closer to her than I was.

My never-ending search for love, combined with the fact that I was working at a mink ranch, gave me a perfect idea. A mink would fit in a cage. I could take a mink to college! I decided to ask my boss if I could buy one of the babies.

The owner of the farm warned me. "You can't tame a mink," he said as I handed him my $25.00.

Maybe *he* couldn't, but I could. Besides, mine was a baby one. It was a tiny animal that had known me since the day it was born. My boss's experience was based on caring for thousands of minks at a time. He'd probably never actually tried to tame one.

At one week old my baby mink was ready to come home. He was still just a tiny thing, about the size of a large hamster. I imagined how awesome it would be if I could train him to curl around my neck. I could wear him in the wintertime like a collar.

The day I brought him home, I went up to my room to play with my new friend. I'd carried him into the house in a box I'd gotten from my boss, so no one would even know I had him in my room. I set the box up on my bed and reached into the box to pick up my beautiful baby mink.

My fingers had barely made it into the box before he chomped down hard enough that when I jerked my hand back, I pulled him right out of the box! I twirled my free hand into the blanket on my bed to cover my fingers, then used my makeshift armor to pry his mouth open and free my fingers.

He immediately started scurrying around my bed, looking for a way down to the floor. I grabbed him by the back of his neck with my good hand as the other hand dripped blood onto my bedspread. He was just scared. I needed to spend more time with him.

After one week and 20,000 bite wounds, the baby mink picked a fight with my cat while I was at work. I came home to find the cat wobbling around with half its scalp peeled away and my baby mink dead. Given just a few more days' growth, the mink would have won the fight against a full-grown cat.

As the summer passed, I learned more about how right the owner of the mink ranch was that a mink cannot be tamed. The power in the jaws of an adult mink could easily overpower a two-hundred-pound dog ... or a two-year-old. One of my co-workers was bitten on the hand by an adult male. The owner, along with two other male farm workers, tried everything they could to pry that mink's jaws apart. In the end, they were forced to beat it to death.

Even though we wore steel-lined leather gloves, we all tended to our daily bite wounds. We had a saying when someone had a bite that went through their gloves: "You're a wuss if you look."

I learned that I am, in fact, a wuss.

I also learned I was wrong.

All my life I had believed anything could be tamed with enough love. I thought of the similarities between my relationship with my baby mink and my mother's relationship with my father. I had tried, unsuccessfully, to tame my mink for two weeks. Mom had tried to tame her untamable animal for twenty-two years.

Maybe Mom and I could both do a better job of heeding warnings.

With our lives moving further away from my father's control, it seemed like he did become tamer. He certainly did everything he could to make Mom believe he was tamer. But just like a mink, you never knew when he'd turn around and snap.

***

It was the middle of summer when Mom came down with a bad case of the flu. Dad took over completely, and I spent more time in my room.

"Just let her sleep," he would bark any time I tried to go into my mother's bedroom to speak to her.

Who the hell did he think he was?

He made dinner for us at night and took care of things like the dishes during the day. He was acting like he should have been acting all along, but that's all it was—an act. He was only acting like a decent person to win Mom back. Once he did, he would turn back into the same wild animal he had always been. He may have made dinner and taken care of Mom, but we didn't need him. My plan was to just bide my time until he was gone.

I was at work the day Mom took a turn for the worse. She was delirious with fever and weak from dehydration when he literally picked her up and took her to the hospital. After emergency surgery, the doctor told us Mom's appendix had ruptured at least two days earlier. He said if dad hadn't brought her in that morning, she would have been dead by afternoon.

Dad had saved her life.

Seemed to me like the least he could do.

Everyone else went on like he was some kind of superhero. Every bad decision he'd ever made was suddenly outweighed by one good one. He was a hero because of his choice not to sit on his ass for once.

I was certainly grateful Mom was alive, but if he had let us take care of her, I would have figured it out eventually. More than anything, I wanted to believe that was the truth, but it wasn't. The horrid truth was, I wouldn't have thought of it. I would have listened when Mom protested a call to the ambulance. Mom would have died if I'd been in charge. Still, that didn't right the wrongs he had perpetrated over the years.

Mom was in the hospital for three weeks. During that time dad was gone a great deal, and I assumed he was up to his old antics. He wasn't. He was with Mom in the hospital.

When Mom finally came home from the hospital, dad's security about his place in our family made him cocky. His infrequent drinking became more frequent, and the kindness left his voice. If he was going to leave, it would have to be because Mom kicked him out again, but she was too kind. I couldn't fathom her telling him to get out of our house.

As it turned out, she never did.

Instead, Mom found dad a place to live that was closer to where he worked. She paid the first few months' rent and set up all the utilities in her own name. Then she told him she'd found him a great place with utilities included.

He was smart enough to take the hint. Dad finally moved out for the last time a few weeks before I went off to college.

The weekend I was leaving for school happened to be the same weekend Mom had her biggest flea market of the year. Even without dad, the antique business was still a lucrative hobby, and she could certainly use the money she would make from the weekend. Most importantly, she couldn't risk not having her spot guaranteed the following year.

I would be moving to school by myself.

On the weekend of the flea market, Mom, Mark, and I spent the days camping in the panel van Mom had purchased after she started doing antique shows.

Usually the shows were reunions with friends I'd known for years—even if I did only see them a few times a year—but we were all growing up. Some of our group had already stopped attending because they'd gone off to college. Some, like my sister, stopped going when they married and started a family; and some just disappeared. Maybe they all felt the same way I did. We'd rather spend the little time we had available with our families than with anyone else. This would be my last flea market as a member of Mom's "immediate" family, and I would miss being part of them.

Sunday afternoon came quickly. Way before I was ready, it was time for me to start my two-hour drive to school. My car was already packed to the roof with everything I would need over the next four months, but I kept stalling by going back over everything I had packed. When I was at serious risk of missing freshman orientation if I didn't get on the road, I rose from my lawn chair.

"Well ..." I said.

"So do you have your ..." Mom went through the list I'd been through a hundred times, even though she was constantly interrupted by people with questions or customers handing her money. Sunday afternoons were the busiest time of the flea markets and Mom didn't have time to chat. Mark was busy with his handheld video game, and I'd already said goodbye to my friends.

I knew that Mom and Mark would be safe from dad, but I still didn't want to leave them.

"Well, I suppose I should get on the road," were the words I said about twenty times. Each time I made the announcement Mom would go back over the checklist of things I needed.

"Do you have the jacket you're going to want to wear if it rains? You might need it before you come home the next time," Mom asked.

"Yup, I packed both of my jackets and my coat," I answered. "I'm all set."

We'd been through the checklist many times, and my 1978 Chevette was already filled to the brim. But then I'd come up with a "stall question" that would give me a reason to stay a little longer with the people I loved most in the world. How could I protect my brother from two hours away if our father came back?

Mom worried about me driving the two hours alone and having no one to help me move into my dorm. I tried to reassure her, but she had customers who'd waited until the end of the weekend to see if she might accept a lower price for one thing or another, and they kept interrupting.

The lump in my throat was so big it physically hurt, and I had no voice. Finally, I climbed into my car and started the ignition. There had been no hugs goodbye as I climbed into my car. My family weren't huggers; in fact, I wondered if anyone except a boyfriend had ever hugged me, excluding events like graduation, of course. I couldn't think of a single time.

As I put my car in drive and waved goodbye to the people who mattered most in my world, I knew the time had come for me to be an adult.

I just had no idea how to go about it.

EVERYTHING I WANTED

By the time I pulled out of the flea market parking lot, I was sobbing uncontrollably. I cried most of my two-hour drive to the city I would call home for the next nine months. I spent the rest of my driving time thinking about who I wanted to be now that I could re-invent myself.

When I pulled onto campus my eyes were burning. I had no idea where I was supposed to go. As usual, I'd done almost nothing to plan for my new adventure. Street signs led me to campus, but none of the buildings had names on them. We would receive maps at orientation, but that wouldn't do me any good if I couldn't find orientation!

Fortunately, there were plenty of pedestrians around to point me in the right direction.

When I finally pulled up in front of my dorm, all I wanted to do was sleep. I was tired from crying. I dreaded the idea of carrying everything from my car up to my third-floor room, and I was nervous about meeting my roommate. As I stood there summing up the best way to tackle unloading my car, I heard a male voice behind me.

"Do you need some help?" An attractive guy who looked extremely familiar was asking if I needed help. He was with an equally attractive friend who also ...

The moment they reached out their hands to introduce themselves, I realized they were Kneips. They were nephews of Mom's boss so I didn't know them well, but they had the same charisma I'd come to love from the rest of their family.

One of them was a smooth-talking player I'd had a crush on for two years, and the other was the son of our former governor.

The last thing I wanted was for either of them to see my face swollen from tears, so I started to protest their help. They insisted they would have my belongings upstairs in no time and started grabbing boxes.

They were right. After a few trips up the stairs, my car was empty, and the cousins were back on their way. I thanked them for their help but made no move to invite either of them into my life.

Most of the girls on my floor were in the hallway to check out the good-looking guys who were helping me move in. They didn't know the guys just took pity on me at the curb rather than specifically coming to help me move, but it helped my reputation anyway. Some of the girls instantly liked me because of the company I appeared to keep. A few instantly hated me. All of them assumed I'd come from a completely different lineage than I had.

And I didn't correct them.

My first week of college went fine. I was finding my way around campus without stopping to ask directions every twenty feet, but I still missed my family. By the time my last class ended on Friday, I was ready to drive home for the weekend.

If I'd known I'd be going home every weekend, I may not have been as verklempt as I had been at the flea market. I liked college well enough, but life at home was finally good and I hated missing out on it. My sister and her husband lived only about twenty miles from Mom. Everyone had stories about the fun things they'd seen my three-year-old and newborn nieces do ... everyone except me. Mom's life without dad blossomed. She ran for school board and won. She studied to be an EMT and volunteered for the local ambulance squad. She was a deacon in our church and a total Type-A parent at my brother's Taekwondo tournaments. Mom had turned the American nightmare into the American dream.

I was still carrying the chip on my shoulder about how bad I'd had things growing up, but the truth was, that segment of my life was over. Everyone I met in college believed I had come from your typical middle-class household. One look at the life my brother and mother led would only confirm that belief. They had no idea I was white trash—and there was no reason for me to enlighten them. My fears of people finding out where I came from began to dissolve, and I was soon proud to invite friends to the house where I'd spent my childhood.

Opening myself up was as foreign to me as it was to my friends.

Every time I went home, I felt more and more like an outsider. It wasn't like my family excluded me from any of the things that were happening. It was just that so many of the memories happened when I wasn't around. I felt like a visitor in a place I no longer belonged.

Occasionally someone would mention seeing dad. Diane took her daughters to see him at least every few weeks, and every so often dad took Mark fishing. They all had stories about his job, his house, or his life. I never had anything to contribute.

Just as he'd always done, my father was able to make me the outsider even when he wasn't around. I hadn't seen my father since he moved out of our house, and I seriously doubted I would ever see him again.

Then one day, just before the end of my first year in college, I did.

I was home for the weekend when dad came to pick up a tool needed to fix his car. I hadn't realized he was there until I went outside. When I saw him, it was obvious his face was messed up. I assumed he had been in a fight. I could hear Mom asking questions, and it was clear she was concerned about him. Something was different about the way Mom was reacting. It wasn't her reaction to a bar fight. I'd heard that reaction many times. My curiosity won the better of me.

Dad was civil when I walked up and even repeated some of the story he'd already told to catch me up to speed. He tried to make light of the scratches and scrapes he had all over his face and arms, explaining he'd gotten them crawling out the window of his totaled car. Apparently, he'd been driving home from the bar one foggy night when he became too "tired" to drive the rest of the way. He pulled over onto the shoulder of the road and turned his car off. He reclined his seat all the way back and went to sleep. When he awoke, the car's roof was flat against his face and chest.

A passing semi had been either driving on the shoulder, or dad hadn't pulled over as far as he thought he had. Either way, the semi drove smack over the top of his car as he slept. He'd even brought Polaroid pictures the police had given him at the scene. Even if I had ever seen his car— which I hadn't—it was unrecognizable from the pictures. It looked like it had gone through a car crusher. There were only a few inches between the top of the doors and the smashed roof. By all accounts, dad should have been dead.

Mom was amazed at how fortunate he was to be lying down when it happened. My brother was fascinated by dad's account of crawling through the broken windshield.

I wasn't amazed or fascinated. *You weren't tired. You were wasted.*

A small part of me winced at the sight of his injuries, but it didn't change anything. He deserved to have his luck finally run out. I told myself the pity I felt was nothing more than being tired of standing alone against him. I gave him my condolences along with everyone else, but the old feelings of not fitting in flooded back as they all added insider comments about his job, his house and everything else I knew nothing about. As soon as there was a break in the conversation I went back inside the house.

He had made me feel like an outsider long enough.

After what seemed a very long time, I heard dad's motorcycle start up. A few seconds later it roared into gear as he sped up the driveway and was gone. He left without saying goodbye—not that I had any delusions he would. He never asked where I was going to college or what I was studying. It didn't matter to him.

I hated him anyway, so it wasn't like I cared. Why should it make a difference to me that he drove past my dorm once a week on his truck route and never even knew I lived there? Why should it matter that I'd never been invited to see where he lived?

We had to live in the same world, but we didn't have to like each other, and that was fine by me. My official stance was that I was still angry and, car accident aside, I couldn't understand why no one else was. Why did my brother look forward to dad coming to take him fishing? Why had my sister wanted him to walk her down the aisle at her wedding? Why did Mom pay all his bills even after they were divorced?

He'd never had to own up to any of the things he had done. He'd never had to answer any of my questions. He'd never even had to say what it was about me that made him hate me so much.

It wasn't fair.

Life was supposed to be fair!

I tried to remind myself it didn't matter. It didn't matter if people I barely knew told me updates about my own father's life when I was in town. It didn't matter that both my brother and sister saw him regularly. He was out of my life, which was exactly what I'd always wanted.

Wasn't it?

FRESH START ON FILTHY SHEETS

During my first year in college, I worked part time, made new friends, and built a life where no one had any idea what my childhood had been like.

I was enrolled in an accelerated registered nursing program that took two years rather than four. Clearly the school had an extra seat to fill, because I wasn't academically qualified to do anything on an accelerated basis. Nightly reading assignments were between two- and three-hundred pages in three of my classes, which meant I was thousands of pages behind by the end of the first couple weeks. Somehow, I bluffed my way through tests and labs well enough to carry a solid C average.

A couple months into classes, my school held a pinning ceremony for first year nursing students. Mom, Mark, Diana and my nieces drove two hours just to see the dean of my college place a pin on my nurse's uniform.

It was 1984 and nursing students wore hard, formed hats bobby-pinned to our heads. Our uniforms included hard, white shoes that took decades to break in, and a polyester dress with white stockings. I stood on the stage with the rest of the first-year nursing students while friends and family took pictures. For the first time in my life, I wasn't worried that my family's presence would embarrass me. I was proud to have them there, and it seemed like they were proud of me in return.

I'd always had friends and dates in high school, but in college people started noticing me for my appearance. In the beginning it was flattering to have attention from guys I didn't know, but I saw myself as a clunky misfit who came from the wrong side of the tracks.

They saw something different, and I no longer knew who I was.

My roommate Darcy had several friends from high school at the college, so from day one I had a social group. We were welcomed to the fraternity and sorority parties during Greek Rush Week. I was invited to join a sorority—as if there were a snowball's chance in hell I could afford to join.

One of the most talked about invitations during Greek Week was to become a Little Sister. I seemed to be the only one in my friend group surprised when the most popular fraternity on campus asked me to be a Little Sister. The problem was, Little Sisters were "White Pants People." They were the girls who went to the grocery store in high heels. They were the girls who would never think of smoking, drinking, or swearing.

More than anything, I wanted to be the lady who vacuums her perfectly white carpet in a perfectly white outfit. I wanted to be the cheerleader who goes on ski trips. My friends showed me how to be exactly that, but the person looking back at me in the mirror was always a fraud. I was Dip Shit, and it was only a matter of time before they figured it out.

I could live with the disappointment of never joining, but could I live with the disappointment of being ousted after they'd already let me in? I didn't think so. Even if I might be able to handle the humiliation, I couldn't take the risk. It was easier to just mock the entire fraternal system and tell myself they were just too stuck up for my taste.

The one thing I did take away from my fraternal experience was my first college boyfriend. I hadn't really noticed him until a group of snotty girls I'd seen at every Rush party started talking about how amazing he was. Without warning, the most important thing in the world for me was to win his affection. I didn't even know I was competitive! It was like proving to the group of snotty girls that I was good enough.

Or maybe I just wanted to prove it to myself.

Dating "The Trophy" introduced me to a whole new world of people I'd never encountered before. He had friends on the football team and friends who played *Dungeons and Dragons*. I didn't need any connection to the cool people beyond knowing him. I finally found my way to fit into the world. I could fit in as a girlfriend. I may have only been a sidekick, but I became someone people wanted to know.

My trophy boyfriend wasn't very happy when an artist friend of a friend asked if I would pose for him. The artist assured my nervous beau that I would be fully clothed the entire time. In fact, my body would be turned into a snake in the final art piece. I saw the painting when it was in the early stages, but I missed the art show where it was unveiled. By the time the show was scheduled, my relationship with "The Trophy" was over and I was once again unsure of my place in the world. If my place in the world was as a sidekick, I certainly couldn't go into the world alone.

***

The drinking age at that time was eighteen, so my friends and I spent a good amount of time in the local bars. One night, a fast-talking stranger came up and asked if I'd be interested in being a card girl for a fight club. He introduced himself and told me he was the promoter who set up the local Golden Gloves tournaments. I'd never heard of the Golden Gloves, but the promoter explained it was an exclusive invitation-only opportunity and stroked my ego until I agreed.

It didn't really take much convincing. I would make $20 for walking around a ring two times a night. Back then, $20 was the equivalent of about six hours work—but there was a downside. I would have to wear a sexy outfit that I felt unbelievably stupid in. As far as sexy costumes go, it was quite conservative. It included a white blouse with long sleeves buttoned to the top, a bowtie, a tuxedo jacket with long tails, and a one-piece leotard. It wasn't nearly as revealing as a one-piece bathing suit, but when you added silky nylons and high heels, the outfit could make anyone look sexy.

The biggest challenge was walking around the ring without falling on my face. Regardless of who I wished I could be, the woman I was wasn't great in high heels.

The first couple of events went well. I didn't stumble a single time. It wasn't really the ring that worried me. The ring was brightly lit and free of obstacles. It was easy to walk in a circle and hold a lightweight card above my head, even in heels. My fear was the metal steps up and down and the cement floor where I'd land.

My fears were unnecessary.

There were always strong, handsome bouncers to help me down the stairs after I walked the ring. From there I went to the dressing room to wait for my next round or get dressed to go home.

Each week narrowed the list of contestants until only two contenders were left. As the fighters dwindled, so did the card girls. I would be the only one walking in the ring during the championship round.

The place was packed when I made my way through the crowd and up to the ring for the third time that night. I no longer minded wearing the outfit, but I hated having people grab at me as I walked through the crowd. I was unsteady enough as it was.

When I walked up the steps to the ring for the last time, the promoter handed me the large card displaying the "round" number. As I walked around the ring with my arms raised above my head, showing the number to the crowd, the lights were even brighter than usual. I could see where I was walking perfectly, but the crowd was invisible beyond the individuals in the first couple of rows. Everything beyond the light poles was completely black. From my vantage point, the crowd didn't seem any bigger than the previous nights, but the noise was deafening.

As I neared the stairs, signaling the end of my walk, one voice stood out loud and clear above the roar of the crowd. "Keep your fucking eyes off my husband, you whore!"

Maybe her voice stood out because of her proximity to the stage, or maybe my ears were just tuned in to angry voices. Either way, she went on … and on.

"You think you're such hot shit? Well, come on over here. I'll show you what hot is!" I had no idea who the woman was screaming at. I was just glad I wasn't a part of it.

I made eye contact with the bouncer as I took his hand and walked down the metal steps for the last time. When I had both feet planted on the cement floor, the bouncer let go of my hand and turned his attention back to the ring.

As the crowd filled in around me, I realized it was much bigger than on any of the previous nights. People stood shoulder to shoulder, and as I tried to nudge my way through, I was wishing the bouncer had escorted me all the way to the dressing room. Every inch I moved meant someone new grabbed at me, but I couldn't move any faster than the mob in front of me would allow.

I heard a familiar angry voice nearby yell something about a "stupid bitch making eyes at my husband." A pang of anxiety struck my heart. I knew the familiar tone of someone who'd had too many drinks and was ready to fight. I just hoped I was far enough away to stay out of the fray. The last thing I wanted was to get caught in the middle of a cat fight.

A sharp sting bit my leg, just before the bouncer pushed his way through the crowd to my rescue. He grabbed me around the waist and pushed the crowd aside, with me in tow. There was no time to stop and see what had stung my leg.

When I finally breeched the perimeter of the crowd, it was a short trip to the dressing room. All I wanted to do was change clothes and go home. I looked down to check the spot on my leg that still stung and saw a round spot that looked like a clump of dirt on my $6.00 nylons. I brushed at it and the stinging sensation fired deeper into my leg. I looked at the edges of the round spot that were clearly melted nylon. The spot was a deep cigarette burn, and I was the "stupid bitch" the woman in the crowd was yelling about. The jealous wife who thought I was making eyes at her invisible husband had ground her cigarette into my thigh. The burned circle of spandex was fused to my leg, and the dark clump wasn't dirt. It was ashes and tobacco.

There had been plenty of people who'd hated me in life, but never out of jealousy. I thought about all the people I'd envied as I picked the charred nylon out of my leg. Would I have ever wanted them to be hurt or disfigured?

My immediate answer would of course be no. Then I remembered my thoughts when I saw my father's cut-up face.

My roommate had come along with me that night, but it wasn't because I was there. The new love of her life was one of the contenders who'd been eliminated in one of the early rounds. Jason was a rough biker type who always looked like he was ready for a fight. It didn't matter if he was in a boxing ring or a bar. He was the cocky loudmouth who was always ready to take on the newest hot shot.

Jason also fit another stereotype I'd come to form. He wasn't anywhere near as strong as he thought he was; and when he lost, he took it out on the rest of the people in his life.

My roommate suffered from lower self-esteem than even I had, and something about him captured her heart. Watching them was like seeing the beginning moments of my parents' love story. In Hollywood, both of their romances would have ended in fairy tale style—the good girl falls in love with the bad boy and her love changes him forever. The only problem? Life isn't a fairy tale. Or a Hollywood movie.

My roommate and her fighter hadn't been dating long before their relationship turned violent.

Jason's parents kicked him out of their house, and he had nowhere to go. My sympathetic roommate asked if it would be alright for him to stay with us for a couple of days and, although I didn't really care for the guy, I hadn't seen his worst side at that point. I also had no ability to say no. I agreed to let him move into our 10' x 10' dorm room.

Nearly every moment of the day, whether I was dressing in the morning or studying for an exam, he was there. College life became reminiscent of my childhood and my main goal was to be invisible. I became privy to every intimate detail of their relationship. Details I didn't want to know, much less see.

Since Jason was a big drinker, they went out nearly every night. Again, reminiscent of my childhood, I was often awoken in the middle of the night to sounds of drunk people coming home.

One night, I was startled awake by name-calling and profanity. At first, I didn't know where I was. My heart started racing, and I instinctively held my breath. I knew I needed to concentrate on my heart to slow it down and make it quieter. I was back in any number of childhood beds, but instead of the angry voices being distant, they were right next to my head, and there was no couch for me to hide behind.

The room was dark but there was enough moonlight coming through the window to make out their shadows. I suddenly knew exactly what was going on. Darcy's fighter boyfriend was taking the fact that he was a loser out on her.

I remained perfectly still in my bottom bunk for several minutes, hoping it would just stop. I could tell from his words and body language it wouldn't. For a long time, it was just the accusations of cheating and lying that my father used to scream at my mother. Their words were so similar—but Jason had never met my father. How could he be using the exact same words? As I pondered the likelihood of some secret script floating around the universe, my mattress slammed against the wall. The fighter slapped my roommate's face— hard—and she fell against my bunk.

I could no longer pretend I was asleep.

I crawled out of bed and walked over to the light switch by the door. When I flipped it on, I saw my roommate crying into her hands as she sat on the floor next to my bunk. Jason looked enraged. Darcy wiped her face and immediately started telling me it wasn't what it looked like. They were just goofing around. She didn't know I'd been awake for several minutes and heard everything he'd said. She also didn't know it wasn't my first night of violence.

"I heard it all," I said in a flat voice.

Embarrassed, and probably scared, Darcy ran out of the room. I assumed she was going to the bathroom, but I didn't go after her. Instead, I stood glaring at the loser she loved.

I sat down at my side of the built-in desk and lit a cigarette. Smoking was allowed in dorm rooms back then. What was I going to say? I just wanted him to leave.

After a few minutes of silence, he started to explain his side.

"She gets so fucking jealous; then she just pushes me and pushes me." He lit his own cigarette and leaned against the wall. "I'm not that kinda guy, you know?"

Huh. There was a script for that too.

My dislike for him turned to utter disgust. I was sick of the guy in every way possible and couldn't care less that he had nowhere to go. My anger wasn't just about him in that moment. It was about every man who ever said the woman he'd beaten made him do it. It was about the fact that I had escaped a world of violence, and he brought it back to me. It was about my absolute hatred of the entire situation.

"I saw what you did. You're nothing but a pathetic loser who couldn't even keep a job working for your dad." I never broke eye contact. My words were filled with every bit of hate I could jam into them. "You are ruining Darcy's life, and the best thing you could do is just get lost." The hatred I felt in my eyes began filling his eyes as well. The more I lectured, the redder his face became, and I saw him clenching his fists.

I didn't care.

Jason reached his breaking point and stomped over to where I was sitting. He raised his fist and cocked his elbow back. It was his preparatory stance to punch me, but I was too angry to be scared.

I looked him in the eye and said, "Go right ahead and do it because I will put you in prison so fast it'll make your fucking head spin." The hate in my voice was obvious, and he must have decided I wasn't worth the risk. I continued to glare at him as he lowered his arm.

The fighter stormed out of the room before my roommate came back from the bathroom, but I knew it was a futile victory. By the following evening they'd made up.

Aside from a few uncomfortable days of not knowing what to say to each other, the night of intervention accomplished nothing. The fighter was still living in our dorm room and my roommate was still madly in love. My disgust at his presence grew, but my roommate begged me to let him stay. He had nowhere else to go and she assured me he regretted everything that had happened.

I knew firsthand that abusers always regretted their actions.

I also knew it rarely stopped them from doing it again.

I didn't want to lose my friend, and it was her room as much as it was mine. Instead of kicking him out, I spent night after night falling asleep to the television to drown out any sounds that might come up in the night.

My roommate's boyfriend had nothing to do during the day except drink and do drugs. By the time I came home from classes, he was always well on his way to passing out. That was fine by me. When he passed out, he was quiet.

One day when I came home from class, I decided to drown my own frustrations in a Mountain Dew. I had one dollar left before payday the following week. The meal plan covered my meals and beverages at meals, so it wasn't like I didn't have food or water. A can of soda pop, however, required cash to purchase. I'd been saving my last dollar for a day when I really wanted to treat myself. I reached into the cup on my desk, but instead of my dollar bill, there was thirty cents. Both my roommate and her boyfriend were in the room.

"Where's my dollar?" I asked no one in particular.

"Oh, Jason needed some change to get a pack of smokes yesterday. I told him you wouldn't mind. I'll pay you back as soon as I get paid," Darcy said, as if it were nothing.

He had taken 70% of my net worth and there was nothing I could do about it. I would not be able to have the Mountain Dew I'd been saving for because someone else took a shortcut and stole it from me.

I was infuriated but there was nothing I could do. Neither of them had any more money than I did.

The final, disgusting straw happened one morning when I awoke.

It started like any other normal morning. I stretched my arms outside the protection of my comforter and rested them on top of my covers but immediately felt moisture soaking both of my arms. I looked up to the mattress directly above my head—the bottom of my roommate's mattress. Over half of it was soaked through with moisture that was dripping on me! I slept through the night with urine dripping onto my blankets! As always, my blankets had protected me from the monsters around my bed, but based on the amount of drippage, they wouldn't last for long.

I had previously complained to my roommate several times about the room smelling like pee, but she insisted the smell came from my guinea pig. I cleaned his cage daily. I even scrubbed Gizmo himself, but the urine smell never went away.

I wiped my urine-drenched forearms with my roommate's towel and stormed toward my closet. She tried to tell me it was because Jason didn't want to go down to the men's bathroom in the middle of the night, so he had been urinating in empty beer bottles.

"He spilled one of the bottles the other night. We thought we'd gotten it all wiped up, but we must have missed a spot," she explained when I questioned her about the soaked mattress. "I'm really sensitive about it too!"

I raised my voice in response to her calm. "The whole room smells like an outhouse! He has peed through your mattress! It is disgusting just walking in the door!"

How many nights had my roommate spent sleeping in a mattress saturated with urine? What did she see in him that made her accept something like that?

Nothing I could say or do was going to make a difference. If I had a problem with Jason being in our room, it was going to be my problem alone.

I grabbed my towel, clothes, the items I would need for the day, my pillow and my pee-soaked comforter. After a couple rounds through the washer and thorough drying, I found a corner of the dorm's TV lounge where I could safely tuck my blanket and pillow during the day. At night I slept on one of the couches.

My roommate may not have been convinced to dump her boyfriend, but I certainly was. All I had to do was survive two months until the semester was over.

I started going home every weekend again and began reconnecting with old friends ... like Tim. By the time the semester ended, I was ready to be as far away from my roommate's filthy secrets as possible.

REALITY BITES

One weekend I brought home a friend from college. We had become closer since I'd started sleeping in the TV lounge, and I couldn't wait to introduce her to my friends—and our favorite club. We had talked a friend into giving Stacy her ID for the weekend because Stacy wasn't quite old enough for the bars. I knew it wouldn't be a problem because Tim was working the door checking IDs. Stacy could have the driver's license of a 90-year-old Nigerian man and still get in—we thought.

My friend and I were likely not the first underaged girls Tim let in the door, but my heart stopped when Tim's boss walked up behind him as he checked Stacy's ID. Not only were we ejected from the club that night, but we also spent the next hour in the parking lot talking to police officers who explained when Stacy would need to be back for court.

Tim felt bad. I felt terrible, and Stacy was as sweet as could be about the whole thing. By the time Tim was off work, my friend and I were ready to go home. It had been a bust of a night, and we were worried about what kind of punishments Stacy was up against.

We agreed to meet at Tim's house the next night to watch movies. Surely that had to be a step in the direction of girlfriend status!

Tim and I spooned on the couch while Stacy sat in a nearby recliner. He kissed my neck and stroked my hair as I tried to focus on the movie. Who was I kidding? I had no idea what movie was playing. I was in heaven.

When Stacy and I left Tim's house that night he asked for my phone number at school, and I gave it to him. We had tentatively made plans to get together the following weekend, and I prayed it wasn't another time where we reverted to periodic couples' skaters.

The week dragged on as I waited for Friday afternoon. My first stop was Traci's to get her opinion on me transferring to Brookings. She not only loved the idea, but she was also renting an apartment with two other girls for the summer, and they needed one more roommate. It would be perfect!

By the time I met Tim at the club for our "date," he was already playing pool with one of his friends. The friend's name was Tina, and although they had never had any romantic interest in each other, my face flushed red. My jealousy just kept bubbling higher as they laughed about shots that went poorly. I wanted to punch her in the face when she touched his arm after something he said made her laugh.

This first time Tim and I were out together on an almost-date, and he had eyes for only Tina. The worst part was that she knew what she was doing. We had bumped into each other several times over the years, and it never went well.

Tina weighed about 350 pounds and worked as a bouncer at one of the other clubs in town. She once threatened me with a butter knife because I wore my letter jacket to a party in another town. She once refused to let me into the club because it was too full, even though people were going in and out all around me. To say the least, she hated me.

I'm sure that played into her flirty behavior as she played pool with my soon-to-be boyfriend. Every time they stood close to each other and talked, she smirked in my direction. When she bent over the table to show her bulbous chest smashed against the felt of the table, she looked at me to be sure I was watching.

The entire time they played, Tim acted as if I were nobody. Oh, he occasionally stopped by the table where Traci and I sat with friends, but only briefly. It didn't matter if he had any romantic interest in Tina. She had his attention, and I was too jealous to handle it.

Traci and I left the club—and I left my heart behind—without telling Tim or even saying goodbye. Clearly, he didn't want a relationship with me beyond making out. The shattered pieces of my heart left behind raw wounds and unanswered questions. My brain kept telling my heart the same answer repeatedly—*He obviously likes her better.*

Once again, the personality flaws that made my father hate me so much became unbearable to someone else. Tim saw the flaws no one would tell me about, and his feelings flipped.

***

My priority became finding a job for the summer. Even without Tim in my life, I wanted to continue with my plans and spend my summer in the apartment with friends. I would be living closer to home with girls who only dated potty-trained men. My-soon-to-be roommates, including my best friend Traci, all attended SDSU. When we gathered one weekend to finalize our lease, their school experiences sounded glorious in comparison to my dive into the underbelly of the "local" versus "college" culture at my school. By the time second semester ended, Darcy was pregnant with Jason's baby.

Everyone was anxious to get checked out of their rooms, and I knew I would have to be present to sign out. When I arrived at the room I'd been paying for but not staying in, Darcy and Jason met me at the door.

"We gotta get on the road now, but here are my keys," Darcy said as she handed them to me. She hugged me and said goodbye.

I was confused. "Don't you have to be here to sign out?"

"Cindy said you could just give her my keys and it would be fine." Darcy grabbed the last box of her things and walked out the door, followed by Jason.

I looked around the empty room and thought of all the memories we had made before Jason came into the picture. Then I saw them: two twin mattresses propped against the bunk bed frame; *both* were saturated with a huge yellow stain. Apparently after I moved to the TV lounge, Darcy and Jason switched to sleeping in my bed.

Our resident assistant Cindy would check out our room and I would have to be the one to explain why two mattresses were saturated with urine. Fortunately, she was not oblivious to the fact that we had a third roommate and that I had been sleeping in the TV room for two months. At one point, she had even asked if I wanted Jason kicked out, but I couldn't do that to Darcy.

Living with "normal" college roommates the next semester would help restore my faith in humanity.

Who was I trying to fool? I was looking forward to a summer of freedom and partying.

I found a job working at a restaurant that was open twenty-four hours. I would make enough to afford rent, and the tips would enable me to cover my social life. Unfortunately, I was by far the worst waitress they had on staff. I was generally scheduled for the worst shifts with the lowest tips. That didn't matter. My mother had taught me what to do when one job wasn't enough. I found a second job selling fireworks. It was a temporary job, but it paid well.

Our apartment was an old house divided in half. There were four male college students who lived on the main floor, while my three friends and I rented the basement.

About a week after we moved in, something went drastically wrong with the sewer system. The smell was atrocious as raw sewage came burbling up every drain in the apartment. By the time the bathtub was about a quarter full, our landlord arrived. In the end it turned out to be a tree root that had grown through the sewer pipes near the street, but it had freaked out one of my roommates enough that she didn't want to live there anymore. Fortunately, we'd all signed separate leases. Her departure just meant more room for the rest of us because she still had to pay her share of the rent.

***

We lived for the weekends and the club where everyone we knew would be on Friday and Saturday nights. It was there that I met the man I would marry.

After the bouncers checked our IDs, my friend Traci and I went up to the bar to get drinks. While we waited in line, we searched through the faces in the room.

That's when I saw him.

Standing by the pool tables was the best-looking guy I'd ever seen in my life. It was hard to tell if he was a real person or a life-sized poster of a model. His blonde hair was perfectly feathered, and his chiseled features didn't just include his face. The crazy thing was that he was looking at me!

I looked away quickly, embarrassed he'd caught me gazing at him, but he kept staring. Traci noticed.

"I think he's looking at you," she said. She'd been my sidekick through high school, and I'd been hers, so she knew instantly what type of guy I liked. We found a table just outside the billiards area. It was close enough to watch him but not close enough to confirm blatant interest. As soon as we sat down, he walked over to our table.

"Would you like to play pool?" He was still looking right at me, but he had to be talking to someone else. There was no way someone so attractive could be interested in someone like me—but he was.

We spent the entire evening talking and playing pool. He didn't expect me to know how to play, but my friend and I had been playing for years. His name was Jerry and by the end of the night I was pretty sure I was in love with him. I gave him my phone number and told him about a barbeque my roommates and I were having at our house the next day. I knew there was no way in the world he'd really wind up coming.

Then he did! From that moment on, we were inseparable.

Jerry wasn't just gorgeous. He came from a family who said a prayer before eating dinner together. No one in his family went to the bar on Christmas Eve to drag his father home. His family was normal. Best of all, he hadn't known me when my family wasn't.

My parents had been divorced for a couple of years by the time I met Jerry. The terrifying days of having friends over on a night when my father decided to pummel my mother were long gone. I was at a point in life where people only knew my history if I decided to tell them. And I had no intention of telling him. The family members Jerry heard about were the ones I was proud to claim.

My sister was pregnant with her third child, so my visits out to the farm were filled with family and close friends. Get-togethers were wonderful. We gathered for every birthday, every holiday, every school event; and no one yelled or hit each other anymore. Dad never made an appearance when the rest of us were together. As far as I was concerned, my father ceased to exist.

Jerry, however, really wanted to meet him, even though I told him from the beginning that just wasn't something that would happen.

As an avid fisherman, Jerry frequently took me on fishing dates. One day while we were out on the shore of our favorite lake, I saw my father in the distance. Dad was busy pulling his boat out of the lake several hundred yards away from us down the sandy beach. We were too far away for him to see our faces, and he wouldn't know Jerry's truck. My father would have no way to recognize me.

I tipped my head in dad's direction and told Jerry, "That's my father."

He wanted to walk over and meet the man he'd heard virtually nothing about, but I said no. "Are you embarrassed to be with me?" Jerry asked.

That was the first time in my life I'd ever heard someone else say something like that. It was the first time I'd ever seen anyone else's insecurities, and my heart went out to him. I confided in him the story of my childhood. I told him the reasons I no longer wanted my father to be part of my life.

Jerry understood, and I didn't introduce the man I loved to my father that day.

Two weeks later, my dad was dead.

BE CAREFUL WHAT YOU WISH FOR

Jerry was a member of the National Guard and had just returned home from his two-week training. Although we had spoken on the phone a couple of times during his absence, I worried the whole time he was gone that he'd realize I wasn't worthy of his attention. When he called as soon as he was in town, I couldn't wait to see him.

I'd prepared a surprise date that included a picnic basket filled with chips, sandwiches, and a bottle of wine. We were going to spend the evening at our favorite fishing spot, so I had everything except the fishing poles waiting in my car. His sister—my co-conspirator—was sneaking those into my car as I chatted with Jerry and his parents.

We were preparing to leave when a knock on their door turned out to be for me. It was Traci, and she was delivering a message from Mom that my father was missing.

"Your mom said his boat had washed up on shore and he wasn't in it," Traci said. "She and Mark will be at your grandma's house."

A million thoughts ran through my mind as I stood there, speechless. He disappeared for days on end all the time. Why was this any different? Most importantly, why should I care?

I had a beautiful evening planned with the man of my dreams whom I hadn't seen in two weeks. The last thing I wanted to do was sit at my evil grandmother's house and talk about where my dad could be. What I wanted to do was have a picnic with Jerry, but Mom wouldn't have sent Traci to find me if she didn't need me.

Jerry didn't hesitate; he insisted on driving me to my grandmother's house where Mom and Mark were already waiting. When we arrived, Grandma seemed to be in shock, so Mom told us everything they knew at that point.

"Your dad went out fishing all day with some friends," Mom said. "They ate dinner at the restaurant, but then your dad wanted to go back out fishing." Mom shook her head in the smallest, slowest movements. "His boat washed up on shore, and they don't know where he is."

Feeling helpless, she said she wanted to go out to the lake to find out what was going on for herself. Again, Jerry stepped in and offered to drive all of us. It was about 11:00 p.m. when we reached the place where my father's boat had washed up on shore.

Jerry, Mom, Mark, and I walked into the bar, and immediately the group of fishing buddies went silent. They had been talking about dad and all looked frazzled with worry. Jerry went to the bar to get us all sodas and took Mark along to help. When they were out of ear shot, Mom started asking the group what they knew.

One of dad's friends was sitting at the end of the table with his head down. Mom was talking to the guys on the other end of the table, so I sat down next to him.

"So where do you think he is?" I asked.

"He's in the lake," dad's friend replied.

The agony on his face showed how much the words broke his heart. All I could do was nod and rub his arm in hopes it would send him the message that everything would be alright. Mom was still engaged in conversation and the guys weren't back with the beverages, so I walked outside alone.

Beyond the parking lot was the beach. As always, I was wearing tennis shoes, so the rocks didn't bother my feet as I made my way to the public boat launch. When I reached the dock where my father would have launched his boat, I walked to the end of the wooden planking and stared into the dark water. The only illumination came from the moon as I stared across the black waters. There were tiny waves whose tips were lit by the moon, making them look like miniature whitecaps. It was beautiful, but I felt like I should be scared.

Had all my years of wishing and praying for his death finally paid off?

I tried to tell myself that my thoughts were ridiculous. Firstly, I wasn't that lucky. Secondly, he was always disappearing for days on end. Sure, he had never had a vehicle show up without him in it, but why did Mom still care so much? Most likely he was just passed out drunk somewhere. Maybe he tied his boat off poorly when he came ashore to sleep off a bender. Maybe some chick he was dating picked him up and he decided he'd take care of his boat later.

No. He had been drinking and fishing for about forty years. It didn't matter what kind of shape he was in; he always managed to load his boat at the end of the day.

The monster was in the lake, and I had put him there.

About the Author

Coleen Liebsch: Author, Entrepreneur, Award-Winning Business Leader, Founder of the Books 4 Kids Program and Public Speaker

Coleen founded her first company in Laramie, Wyoming. From a KOA on the outskirts of town, to nine employees, Tri-Tech Marketing filled a need other marketing companies overlooked.

In 2016, Coleen founded a non-profit called the Books 4 Kids Program where she provides character-building books to children from PK to 8th grade, for free. So far, the organization has given out over 50,000 books in eleven states and four countries.

Coleen's first novel, a thriller titled *Choices: Arrival of the Fourth Generation,* was a 2017 finalist for the McGrath House Indie Book Awards.

Coleen lives in Eastern South Dakota with her husband and their pack of Pomeranians.

If you would be interested in Coleen speaking to your group, please visit www.coleenliebsch.com for more information.

Other books by Coleen include:

Thank You for Abusing Me Book 2: Why Did She Stay?
Choices: Arrival of the 4th Generation
Judgment Day
Invisible Victim

Children's books written as "Goob"
A Fairy Different Life
The Color of Beauty
A Day In The Life
Why Don't I Fit In?

Dear Reader,

Thank you for investing your time in this book. I sincerely hope you've enjoyed my story... so far. In fact, I would love to hear your opinion through a review! I read and reflect on each, and every comment, to help me grow as an author. Thank you, in advance, for sharing your thoughts and insights!

The conclusion of Thank You for Abusing Me is titled Why Did She Stay. In this book, I will share the steps, mis-steps and flat out falls encountered on my journey to learn why my mother would stay in an abusive relationship... and why I would.

If you find yourself in a situation where you are afraid for your safety, regardless of the reason, help is available! Please call **800-799-7233**. No one should live in fear.

Take care of each other, and I hope to see you in person soon!

Coleen

www.ingramcontent.com/pod-product-compliance
Lightning Source LLC
Chambersburg PA
CBHW061758070526
44586CB00023B/2617